HarperCollins books may be purchased for educational, business, or sales promotional use. For information, please email the Special Markets Department at SPsales@harpercollins.com.

Fox News Books imprint and logo are trademarks of Fox News Network LLC.

FIRST EDITION

All Scripture quotations, unless otherwise indicated, are taken from the Holy Bible, New International Version®, NIV®. Copyright ©1973, 1978, 1984, 2011 by Biblica, Inc.™ Used by permission of Zondervan. All rights reserved worldwide. www.zondervan.com. The "NIV" and "New International Version" are trademarks registered in the United States Patent and Trademark Office by Biblica, Inc.™

Photo credits for the insert artwork:
Pages 1, 8–9, 16: istock.com/Lev Liulchuk
Pages 2–7, 12–15: @tanyadzo/stock.adobe.com
Pages 10–11: @Lasa/stock.adobe.com

Designed by Nancy Singer

Library of Congress Cataloging-in-Publication Data has been applied for.

ISBN 978-0-06-322593-0

22 23 24 25 26 LSC 10 9 8 7 6 5 4 3 2 1

Faith

STILL MOVES MOUNTAINS

MIRACULOUS STORIES OF THE
HEALING POWER OF PRAYER

HARRIS FAULKNER

Faith

STILL MOVES
MOUNTAINS

ALSO BY HARRIS FAULKNER

9 Rules of Engagement: A Military Brat's Guide to Life and Success

Breaking News: God Has a Plan

To my husband, Tony, and our two daughters, Bella Grace and Danika Jo, thank you for teaching me every day that life's adventures require my unconditional love for the Lord and bravery to live out His purpose for me.

"Truly I tell you, if you have faith as small as

a mustard seed, you can say to this mountain,

'Move from here to there,' and it will move.

Nothing will be impossible for you."

—MATTHEW 17:20

CONTENTS

CONTENTS

Restoration

Perseverance

Healing

Faith

STILL MOVES
MOUNTAINS

INTRODUCTION

*Y*ou are divinely loved. If you haven't heard that today, read that out loud. You are so loved that God created, sacrificed, and resurrected His only son for you. It is also true that life is hard. And often it's easy to forget the power of prayer, relationship with God, and faith. This loss of faith is all around us. And it's contagious.

Journalists see people at both their best and their worst. Murders, rescues, robberies, reunions: we're there to cover all of them. In my quarter century on the job, I've seen some people blessed with miracles and others devastated by what can only be described as the work of the Devil. Some people pray for dreams that then come true. And there are random tragedies that turn others inside out with pain and hopelessness. I've witnessed people coming back from the brink over and over.

Through all of it, the one constant is God's presence.

God is with us when we are at the lowest of our lows and the highest of our highs. He's there at every point in between. Sometimes He makes Himself known to us in the most obvious of ways; sometimes in a quiet whisper. But always He's there, one prayer away.

This is a book about the power of prayer. It's about how God comes alongside us in our daily lives. He can bring us through any valley, be it a struggle with illness, depression, or death—or just a bad day. This book is full of stories reminding us that God sees and cares when we're struggling; miracles that provide the most visible evidence of God's greatness and grace; proof that prayer isn't just words—it's action.

We need reminders of that now more than ever.

One of the primary reasons why we are people of faith is that it helps to restore a sense of order in the chaotic world in which we live. A number of stories in this book deal with people who have found themselves subject to circumstances that overwhelmed their sense of order.

In many cases, they were, through no fault of their own, dealing with the random nature of tragedy. There's the story of the Alabama grandmother who survived a severe F4 tornado that ravaged her town. The one room in her house which survived, was her prayer closet. Even still she praised God, preaching His goodness to her family and community. I've covered a number of stories over the years when the randomness of destructive forces has devastated one family and left another untouched. And, in a number of instances what explained why one house survived and another didn't, was the role of faith and prayer. It is a hard fact that people may not succeed in every circumstance because God has a plan. But, the positive impact of faith and prayer on outcomes is frequent enough that I believe that it is the common denominator of miracles.

Increasingly, Americans don't believe that. In 1944, the Gallup public opinion organization began asking Americans if they believed in God. The number was astoundingly high, nearly 100 percent. And each time it took that poll in the 1950s and the 1960s, the percentage of Americans who said they believed in the Lord remained in the same range.

Then something changed. We became less likely to say we believed in God and even less likely to have faith that God intervenes in our lives. Most recently, in May 2022, Gallup announced that currently only 81 percent of Americans believe in God. Digging deeper, only four in ten people surveyed told Gallup they think God does anything on our behalf. No miracles, no answered prayers.

That's not true. But that kind of despairing thinking can replicate faster than a virus. In a world in which our reminders of God are few, it's even easier to have to grapple with doubt. It's unclear where we're headed as a more secularly focused society pushes our future generations to ignore the power of prayer. Now is a perfect time to push back on the notion that God doesn't intervene in our lives; to remember that prayer is as powerful as ever; that faith does indeed still move mountains.

That doesn't mean God always acts in the way we hope or in our timing. As James 1:19 states, "My dear brothers and sisters, take note of this: Everyone should be quick to listen, slow to speak and slow to become angry." That last point is particularly important. Many of us find silence uncomfortable. When we think that God is silent, when we believe that He has forgotten us, when we think that He hasn't heard us, it is easy to get angry. We may not take it out on God, we may not be angry with Him, but we may be angry with ourselves and our perception that His silence is a result of our being unworthy. The question that is on the lips of many people throughout history in troubled times is "Where are you, God?"

The stories in this book are a reminder that He is with us at all times. And many of them also offer encouragement for those of us struggling with the silence of God. We may not know the hour or the means by which He will answer our prayer. Sometimes the answer will be silence. And in that pause, we are many times able to answer our own questions, resolve our own problems. Throughout this book we'll examine stories of miracles, and discover that God speaks in many other ways, too.

As a parent, I know that it is hard to see my children struggle with anything. But seeing them find solutions to their own problems is extremely rewarding. As our Heavenly Father, God has to measure out His degree of involvement. We are beings possessed with free will, and what choices we make are our own responsibility. In these stories, we see God at work, giving us the freedom we need and intervening at the most critical times to save us from ourselves. We receive the opportunity to learn and go on learning. Prayer isn't just about receiving a blessing from God, having Him answer a request. Instead, it is a back-and-forth exchange of questions and answers.

We also learn, no matter how afraid we are, how abandoned we feel, how much we think our Father has turned away, that He will never leave us alone. From an American pastor Andrew Brunson falsely imprisoned in Turkey to little Nancy Owen abandoned on the streets of her hometown to Tina Zahn, a mom locked in depression, I have found story after story of people who realized that God was with them, even when they didn't know it at the time.

We usually think of prayer as something which makes us strong. But the surprising thing about prayer is how it reminds us we are vulnerable, mortal, and needy. And that is a gift, because in our weakness we can see God's great strength. Throughout this book we'll see time and again, examples of God working through us when we're at our most helpless. After all, the son of God Himself became helpless to accomplish salvation.

Often when delivering commencement addresses and inspirational speeches to young audiences, I remind them that we are all like IKEA furniture—assembly required. I've had to mature in my faith and in how I conduct myself in my relationship with God. The Harris of 2022 is not the same Harris of 1992 or 1982. The same is true of my relationship with the Holy Spirit, with Jesus, and with God the Father. God has seen me at my worst, He's seen me at my best; that's part of the deal of being His creation.

But God did make me for a purpose. I believe that God's assignment for my life is to be a witness. That is my calling, and in sharing these stories and by witnessing so much, I am compelled to help others see that even in the midst of so much that seems chaotic and random, there is order. We may not see it in the moment, but it is there. I believe that we all need reminders of this, especially because of what we all continue to endure. The ongoing COVID-19 pandemic, the rise in mass killings, war, economic downturns, and other events challenge us daily. In the face of all this, too often, hope fades. My wish is that as you read these stories of God's direct intervention in people's lives, hope will bloom again in your heart.

Ultimately, I hope that this book will serve as a source of answers and comfort. I also hope that it will make you ask questions; that it will lead you toward a deeper understanding and appreciation of God's mysteries. I urge you to read this book in reflective moments. Embrace the quiet, and let the wisdom behind God's works speak to you. God wants us to be curious. He wants us to seek greater knowledge. He wants us to sit comfortably in silence and know that He is the one true answer.

There are things that happen to the soul when the weather moves in. It is the hand of God. You cannot control it. We remember then how fragile we really are. Stories of prayers answered in the midst of such scenarios remind us that God is God over nature. He created this world and holds it in the palm of His hand.

Rescue

That's why the psalmist wrote:

> By the word of the Lord the heavens were made,
> their starry host by the breath of his mouth.
> He gathers the waters of the sea into jars; he
> puts the deep into storehouses.

—PSALM 33:6–7

AND ALL THE PEOPLE SAID AMEN!

High school seniors on a fun outing run into trouble that only God can solve.

> In my distress I called to the LORD; I cried to my
> God for help. From his temple he heard my voice;
> my cry came before him, into his ears.
>
> —PSALM 18:6

"We could make it."

Heather Brown looked across the swirling waters of Matanzas Inlet. For a moment she hesitated, sizing up the distance to swim out to the inlet, but then echoed back her friend Tyler Smith's prediction.

"Yeah. Yeah, let's do it."

It was senior skip day in April 2019, and Heather and Tyler had joined their fellow classmates to play hooky on the beach. Located on the Atlantic Coast, on the north side of the Matanzas Inlet, Vilano Beach is considered one of St. Augustine's best-kept secrets. It's a strand so hidden away that the college spring breakers don't even know to flock to it, and that day, with the winds up and the waves high, the group from Christ Church Academy had nearly the entire stretch to themselves.

It had been a great day, and Heather felt a thrill as they jogged across the blazing white sand of Vilano Beach and entered the water. It was going to be so cool, she thought, when she and Tyler were the first ones to make the swim to the inlet.

What the two seventeen-year-olds didn't know was that the National Weather Service had issued a small-craft advisory for the day.

A typical NWS marine weather message like this would read, "Wind and wave conditions will be hazardous for small craft. Inexperienced mariners, especially those operating smaller vessels, should avoid navigating in these conditions."

Despite the conditions, the two teens, who'd been friends since fourth grade, decided to swim across the St. Augustine Inlet from Vilano Point to Anastasia Island, a distance of five hundred yards. They were athletes at the school, but neither was a competitive swimmer, and in what Heather described as a "pride moment," they decided that they were both in good enough shape to make the crossing, hoping to impress their friends. A third student, Heather's neighbor, joined them.

There were no lifeguards stationed along that remote stretch of the beach.

Tyler and Heather had no way of knowing how a series of decisions they made would put them on course for a miracle rescue. But their prayers were answered in such an improbable way that it changed not just their lives but a total stranger's. God's provision always deserves a resounding "Amen!" yet in this case, it was a literal "Amen" that He delivered to the right place, at the right time, under the worst of circumstances for two teens who'd made a disastrous decision.

But all of that was in the future. For the moment, Heather, Tyler, and their friend swam along confidently.

At first their goal was modest—to reach a red buoy that sat bobbing in the water less than a hundred yards away. As they swam toward it, it appeared as if the buoy had become unmoored. Instead of closing the gap on the ocean marker, the kids were being tugged farther and farther from it. The trio was reduced to a duo. Doubting his ability to navigate the waters, the third student turned around and returned to the beach. Caught in a strong Atlantic Ocean current, the remaining two were suddenly victims of forces they couldn't see but could feel.

That was when Tyler decided that a change of plans was needed. He recognized that not just the land but the buoy as well were both impossible destinations to reach. As they rose and fell with the swells, the beach was barely visible. Back on the coast, their friends were trying to catch a glimpse of the pair but couldn't.

Tyler later told reporters that at that point, he decided that he and Heather should point themselves toward a known landmark: in this case, rising above the waves' crests, St. Augustine Lighthouse.

They were done with heading any farther out to sea. It was time to return to the safety of the shore. But again the current worked against them. Try as they might, the pull of the water took them farther out to sea.

Heather's thoughts, through the haze of increasing terror, were focused on what would happen when they got back. "I was worried that I was going to be in trouble for doing this," she said.

Senior skip day coincided with her younger sister's birthday. That evening, the family had plans to celebrate, and Heather and Tyler's activities threatened to make the party impossible.

She would soon realize that their problems were much bigger than a postponed party.

"We started to realize we were getting further away from the lighthouse rather than getting closer," Tyler later told a local news outlet. "That's when we started to freak out."[1]

Heather realized that the current had pushed them so far out that reaching the lighthouse was impossible.

A God's-eye view of the scene would have shown two tiny dots in the vast expanse of slate gray, white-capped water. It might have looked like a movie. To God, such a scene is calm. When Jesus' disciples were crossing a lake in Galilee and a storm sprang up, they must have been astonished by His calmness. What they didn't understand was that He had a God's-eye view. He was not afraid of a storm because He could calm it in an instant.

Tyler and Heather had no such ability. It's easy to imagine the rising panic that quickened their hearts and unsettled their nerves.

Making little to no progress toward the lighthouse, they began to wonder if they would make it back to shore. They were treading water and trying to swim. And time was working against them. The minutes ticked by, and soon they had been in the water for an hour. People can tread water for longer than you might think, but doing it in rough seas is another matter entirely.

As the teenagers looked around, they saw only open water. Given the marine warning, no boats were in sight. Typically, only a few pleasure craft passed through the inlet anyway, so that day, they had little hope of being rescued. As the weather worsened,

Heather and Tyler were surrounded by a miles of angry gray ocean.

Now, they were running out of time.

WEEKS EARLIER, ERIC WAGNER HAD also become very conscious of time slipping away too quickly. It was about to become necessary to move his home. His home was a yacht.

Years before, Eric had purchased a 1977 Hatteras motor yacht, fifty-three feet in length and capable of sleeping up to six people in three cabins. Since he worked in software, he was able to work from anywhere in the country. For years, he had kept the craft at a marina in Delray Beach, Florida.

"It was my home away from home," he said, and during the winter he lived aboard it, anchored in that marina. The rest of the time he spent in New Jersey with his family. He'd had no intention of leaving Delray Beach. Then he had received short notice that the owners of the marina were undertaking massive renovations that would last as long as eight months. He would have to find a new marina in which to dock his boat.

Eric found himself in a dilemma. He hadn't planned to go back to New Jersey right then, but his winter hideaway was suddenly no longer a possibility. Finding another slip in which to dock was proving to be difficult. Finally, he decided that he would instead run the boat up to New Jersey.

But that created more problems. Though aficionados considered the Hatteras a classic, at forty-two years old, it was in need of repair and regular maintenance. Busy with managing his own company, Eric didn't have the time to complete all of that work, and with the clock ticking on his rented space at the marina, he had to spring into action.

He plotted the course. The thousand-mile voyage would take ten days. He asked three friends to join him for a trip that was to start in early April. A trip of that length, especially in a boat of that vintage, required lots of preparation time—something he didn't have due to the imminent construction project. And as we've all experienced from time to time, little delays turned into longer ones. A part that Eric was told would be in stock wasn't. Customer service wasn't much help. Eric's stress level rose, and frustration set in. It wasn't just getting out of the marina in time that increased his sense of urgency; he needed to get going before the storm season kicked in.

"There's a lot of work that has to be done to make sure you have all pieces and parts running perfectly," Eric explained. "We were running up against poor weather that was only going to get worse as we got into the springtime. It's not the time you want to travel the Atlantic coast. So I was trying to figure out how to get out of there as quick as possible and thread that needle to get up north before the weather got too bad. And it's not necessarily just the weather. The seas themselves are rougher in the spring, because the Gulf Stream going one direction, the winds blowing another, creates a lot of turbulence that isn't there during the fall or the summertime, which are much more comfortable to travel in."

Despite all the obstacles they faced, they managed to leave Delray Beach on April 16. However, in their rush to do all the pre-trip preparations, they'd skimped on one of the patches they'd applied to the fiberglass hull, and it failed. The yacht started taking on water. Fortunately, it didn't have to be taken out of the water to do the repairs, and five hours after pulling into a marina to redo the patch, they were under way the next morning.

It was then that Eric noticed that the diesel engine wasn't as responsive as it should have been. A quick look at the fuel tank revealed the source of the problem: a buildup of algae. Another round of repairs was necessary to replace filters. By the time they reached the Jacksonville area on the seventeenth, they were a day behind. At least, to that point, the weather had been favorable.

The following day, the eighteenth, the craft was in good repair, but the weather was bad. A small craft advisory was in effect. Eric estimates that the winds were gusting at thirty to forty knots—thirty-four to forty-six miles per hour. In a tiny inlet they could see whitecaps on the waves. Still, Eric was eager to take advantage of the fact that the wind was out of the south, pushing them. The boat could travel at high speeds out on the ocean, and with the tailwind they could make up some of the lost time.

Eric discussed their options with his companions, friends from New Jersey named Troy Tennis and Wayne Savage and a friend from Florida named Richie Petrusyk. Everyone but Eric believed that the wisest choice would be to forgo moving out into the open waters of the ocean. The risk to their comfort and safety would be greater than the reward of higher speeds. Yes, they were behind schedule, but how much farther would they fall behind if they encountered real difficulty in the troubling waters? Still, Eric was the captain and owner. The decision was his to make, and they'd support it. Knowing that he had limited time before he needed to return to his business in New Jersey, Eric opted to roll the dice. At fifty-three feet in length, the boat was structurally capable of running in such waters.

There's capable and then there's comfortable. Eric soon learned that the open-seas decision wasn't the best option. The violent water had the boat bouncing around; it was so rough that objects were dancing in the cabin. Judging discretion to be the better part of valor, they decided to abandon the idea of going out to the Gulf Stream for their northbound journey. Instead, they would use the slower but calmer Intracoastal Waterway, which essentially hugs the shoreline. They were miles from the next inlet that would help them gain access to the ICW, so, instead of cruising four miles out from the coast, they stayed closer, just two miles offshore.

Satisfied that they'd at least given the open-ocean option a shot, they settled in for the run to the inlet. They figured they might as well make the best of a bad situation. They gathered on the flying bridge, a smaller open platform atop the main bridge equipped with a secondary set of navigational controls. Unlike many flying bridges, it was enclosed with a canvas roof and plastic (isinglass) windows. In the gusty winds, all those materials were rattling, adding to the noise. The original sales brochure had boasted that the craft had the latest in 1970s infotainment—a stereo tape system that was piped throughout the boat. The system had been upgraded, and the four men enjoyed listening to music above the sound of the wind, the loud thrum of the engines as Eric throttled up in order to get the bow of the boat to better plow through the rough seas. Their mood was high-spirited despite the rough seas. The sky was nearly cloudless, and the bright sunlight and wonderful visibility were a balm counteracting the difficulties they'd encountered over the last days. From their position high above the waterline, the distant shore was visible. Knowing that the decision had been made for them to return to the calm waters and having the shore in sight were a comfort. They were going to make the best of a bad situation.

As it turned out, their decision to go out onto the open ocean, however briefly, along with all the other delays, would eventually put the yacht into the right place at the right time to answer the teens' prayers.

HEATHER HAD CHOSEN A BIBLE verse for graduation. It reads, "We rejoice in our sufferings, knowing that suffering produces endurance and endurance produces character and character produces hope. And hope does not put us to shame because God's love has been poured into our hearts to the Holy Spirit and has been given to us." (Romans 5:3–5)

Endurance and hope were ideas that resonated strongly with her as an athlete. If the two students were adrift that day, that certainly wasn't the case with the rest of their lives. They were about to graduate in a month, and Heather had been accepted at Embry-Riddle Aeronautical University, where she planned to be a naval ROTC marine officer. Her ultimate goal was to become a Marine Corps pilot.

For his part, Taylor was headed to Florida Atlantic University to study business finance. He planned to get his pilot license and join the air force. Though there are no guarantees in life, the two seemed to have a strong foundation in faith and service that held them in good stead.

Their lives were full of hope and dreams. But their endurance was about to be tested by suffering. Just after Romans 5:3–5 is a verse that reminds us that although our endurance may be tested by suffering, it was when we were powerless that Jesus came to save us. That was about to prove true for Tyler and Heather.

The thought of dying didn't enter Heather's mind. She just thought, *No, I have to keep swimming. I have too much that I'm supposed to be doing. I'm supposed to graduate. I'm supposed to go to my sister's birthday dinner tonight. I'm supposed to be on the volleyball team. I'm supposed to be in the Marine Corps. There's no way this ends now.*

Somehow, she wasn't physically tired. "My adrenaline was

through the roof. I didn't feel the cold until near the very end. I never had an image of drowning."

There was little to comfort Tyler and Heather. They rose and fell on the ocean swells, never rising high enough to see the shoreline. All around them were water and the sky above. Then, nearly two hours into their ordeal at sea, Tyler's muscles began to cramp. He clung to Heather, and, arms linked, they kept each other afloat and prevented themselves from drifting apart.

"If we kept swimming, we would have drowned," Heather later said.

They began to pray.

Tyler would later recall to news reporters, "When we linked arms, [I] honestly cried out to God, 'If you're out there, please send something to save us.'"[2]

The kids then saw something that made them both scream.

ABOARD THE YACHT, THE FRIENDS were laughing and talking. The ride was still rough, but they knew that it wouldn't last much longer. Soon, on their northerly journey, they would turn west toward the inlet that would take them to the ICW and calmer water.

The yacht had the ocean to herself. "All the fishing vessels go out to the Gulf Stream because you get a free ride," Eric said. "If you want to go north, you ride the current. And then you get to ride the wind heading back south."

At one point, above the noise of the wind and the motor and the music, the passengers thought that they heard something. "Somehow, we thought we heard a scream. We all stopped talking. We looked around."

All around they saw nothing but ocean and sky. Seeing nothing, they attributed the sound to seabirds. They carried on talking.

A moment later, they heard the sound again.

Troy, who was behind the wheel, didn't hesitate. He jerked the wheel hard left, shouting, "There's people back there!"

Eric looked back over his shoulder as the boat came about. "About two hundred yards behind us, I saw two little dots," he said later. "One of them was waving."

Tyler and Heather, spotting the yacht, had begun screaming, desperate to catch the attention of the crew.

Troy continued to turn the boat around hard, heading in the direction of what they'd heard and now seen. All four men had years of boating experience. They knew what to do in case of a rescue. Troy kept piloting from the fly bridge, and Richie stayed with him to serve as a lookout. Eric and Wayne ran down to the bow of the boat. There on the lower deck they grabbed life vests and rope that were stowed there in case of such an emergency.

From their vantage point, they only occasionally got a glimpse of the young people in the water. In between those brief sightings, they consulted with the other two men. The roaring wind made it nearly impossible to hear, so they communicated through hand signals and pointing. Eric and Wayne had tied ropes to the life jackets. In seas like that, it was potentially dangerous to get too close to the victims in the water. Not only could the boat slide sideways and expose the people in the water to the propeller, but they could be slammed into by the hull.

Troy continued to pilot the boat, creeping up on the two as skillfully as he could. Eventually the boat was positioned so that Eric and Wayne could toss the life jackets in the direction of Tyler and Heather. They worked their way toward them and held on. As he hauled on the line, Eric shouted, "Where's your vessel?"

He believed that the only way the pair could have been that

far out in the ocean was if they had been on some small craft, a sea kayak or such that had overturned. There was no other plausible explanation.

Exhausted, bobbing up and down, Heather was barely able to respond, "I'll tell you later!"

That's when Eric realized the full extent of the seriousness of their condition. He could see it in Heather's eyes and hear it in her voice. Tyler wasn't speaking at all. Both teenagers wore pained, fearful, wide-eyed expressions. With the motor cut and riding sideways to the waves, the boat rocked relentlessly. How would they get them on board in their condition? Eric hoped that the pair would be able to climb the ladder to the swim deck, the platform closest to the waterline which they could access with a ladder.

His heart in his throat, he watched as they maneuvered themselves toward the ladder and then clung to it. He had no idea how long the two of them had been in the water and how weak they'd become. They couldn't pull themselves up the ladder. Realizing that, Eric and Wayne rushed down to them and helped haul them aboard. As Eric pulled and Wayne pushed Heather aboard, Eric said, "She looked me square in the eye and said, 'God is real.'"

Stunned, all Eric could say was "I know."

The two men assisted the drenched teens in getting onto the main deck.

"We could tell they were in tough shape. Their lips, his lips especially, were white, and they were shivering uncontrollably," Eric recalled. He was afraid that hypothermia was setting in. He and his friends provided towels for the two to wrap themselves in.

"Do you have a boat?" Eric asked. He was still wondering how they could have gotten out that far.

"No," Tyler said finally through chattering teeth. "We were swimming."

Eric shook his head in disbelief. "How long have you been out here?"

"I don't know," Heather said. "I have no idea what time it is."

Eric told them that it was nearly one o'clock.

She did the math. "Two hours."

Eric's jaw dropped. Two hours in water like that must have felt like an eternity, he thought.

Very worried about the kids' condition, Troy fired up the engines again to stop the boat from rocking so hard from side to side, while Wayne called the Coast Guard. None of the four crew members was a medic, and they thought it might be best to get the kids onto a Coast Guard vessel. Eric led them into one of the cabins and gave them blankets to help insulate them and keep in their body heat. Rich heated water in the microwave for them to drink to help bring their body temperature up.

Within a few minutes, Eric noticed that Heather and Tyler had started to get their color back. Eric had never seen anyone with stone white lips before. He wondered how much longer the two of them might have been able to last in the water. Their shivering lessened, and they recounted what they'd gone through.

"Out of desperation, we started to pray—" Heather said.

"I started to call out to God," Tyler cut in.

Eric wondered what the young man meant. Tyler continued, "And that's when you showed up."

"The name of my boat is the *Amen*," he told them.

They all fell silent. The reality of all that had taken place and the significance of that brief exchange settled over them all.

"It got emotional, and it was just kind of overwhelming, how crazy that whole moment was," Eric recalled. "I'm a man of faith. I knew that they were people of faith as well. I told them that and had to catch my breath. I was choked up about it. So the gravity of the situation kind of sunk in. At that moment, these guys were really close to death." The two teens began crying.

The *Amen* was soon setting course for a rendezvous with a Coast Guard rescue boat. Very soon, the pair was reunited with their family and friends. Eric and his friends continued on. Once under way toward New Jersey, they realized that they didn't even know the last names of the two teens they'd rescued. Only after Eric posted on Facebook about the experience did the media pick up on the story.

Later, Tyler explained what he had meant about his calling out to God. "I cried out: 'If you really do have a plan for us, like, come on. Just bring something,'" he told a reporter for WJAX, a CBS affiliate in Jacksonville. ". . . From us crying out to God, for Him to send someone for us to keep living and a boat named 'Amen,' there's no way that it wasn't Him."[3]

Their school, Christ's Church Academy, issued a statement on Facebook, calling the rescue miraculous, and saying "The staff, students and families of Christ's Church Academy are incredibly grateful for God's protection over Heather and Tyler." They also expressed their gratitude to Eric and his friends.

In considering all that had led to the rescue, Eric later told reporters, "The young couple was gracious and grateful to us and to God. It was the latter all along." Also, as he later put it, "We had no business being out there."

As it turned out, they were doing God's business.

Eric reflected on all the circumstances that had contributed to their being in the right place at the right time, how the boat had first gone past the pair, and then, with the wind coming from behind, their voices had been carried over the wind and water and audible above all the noise aboard the *Amen*.

"I believe it was miraculous. There were too many coincidences, in my opinion, for this to be a coincidence," he said. "I truly believe it was divine intervention. It had nothing to do with me. I was just put there at the right place at the right time, and I did the same thing anyone else would have done, pulled them aboard."

He added, "There's no radar sensitive enough to pick up two heads bobbing in the water. We didn't have the radar on. We only run it at night. We just go visual during the day. We were out there in the clear middle of the day in bright sunny skies. There was no problem with visibility that day, but it's amazing how things disappear out there. You're in a vast blue sea. You can't pick up small things, like a buoy or a marker, not unless you're really looking for them."

Eric also reflected on the significance of the name of the boat. He hadn't named it the *Amen*, the previous owner had, and when it had come time to repaint the boat after Eric had purchased it, he had considering renaming it. For some reason, he was unable to come up with one that he liked. He stuck with *Amen*. He now says that he will never change the name of the vessel.

Heather has since had time to further reflect on the events and the role it played in her life. She said, "I've grown up in a Christian household. So I've known that, obviously, God is there for you. But I've had that idea thrust at me for a long time through going to a Christian middle school and high school. It gets to a point where that just becomes background noise. But having this experience and being a literal firsthand witness to God just rescuing me like that, and way too many things that shouldn't have happened happening, and seeing the name of the boat, there was no doubt that God had handpicked me out of the ocean and rescued me. In the Bible, it literally tells you that God is your rescuer. And that weekend was also Easter. Our pastor talked about how God is our rescuer, and I was losing it. I actually experienced that truth. I had an eye-opening experience that told me that God being a rescuer is for real. It isn't just something I heard about."

Whether it is active moments of doubt or simply taking for granted God's greatness and his compassion for all of us, we've all likely experienced what Heather had in thinking of the Gospel as "background noise." Daily life and our own concerns become distractions. Since her rescue, Heather has experienced that drifting from God as well. She admitted, "Freshman year of college was a little rough. I was doing so many things. I was playing volleyball. I was doing Marine Corps ROTC. I was a freshman, bottom of the barrel, so I had to do everything for those groups. I had to adjust to college academics. I was spreading myself too thin and not making good choices. This was my first experience with real freedom. It was nice being on my own and getting to make my own decisions, but I didn't make the best ones."

She experienced another perspective shift, one that many young people do: "I guess I got, in quotation marks, 'rescued' again after freshmen year. Everything got put in perspective when COVID-19 hit. I was like, 'Man, what have I done with my life, my whole year of schooling?' I decided I didn't want to be like this. I know better than this. I saw how God was in my life. I needed to show that. I just kind of reminded myself that I got rescued for a reason. I needed to do things differently."

A part of the miracle of Heather and Tyler's rescue is the fact that they stayed afloat for as long as they did. God's strength was transfused into Heather. "It's funny," she observed. "Now, as part of my ROTC training, I have to do different qualifications. One of them is in the pool. Now I've been taught how to tread water properly and how to prone float and how to save my energy. I didn't know any of that before, and it's ironic learning it after the fact. Even treading water in the pool now, I think back and I wonder, 'How did I do that?'"

The answer, of course, is that through God, all things are possible. He brought together three people, and transformed their lives, and set into place an example for all of us to learn from.

Eventually, Eric did speak with Heather and Tyler. Their parents were also in touch to thank him. To this day, on the anniversary of the near tragedy, Heather's father sends Eric a note of thanks. (Heather now teases her sister by saying that the day is no longer her "birthday" but "our day.") Eric believes that as a man of God, he and his family have been blessed in many, many ways.

Still, as he said, "I have anxiety and stress like everybody else. I can meditate and talk with God, and I feel better. And I've yelled at God before in the past when things went wrong. I apologize and realize He's got a much bigger picture that I don't understand. And He forgives me immediately, and I know that. So I've lived a life of forgiveness. I've been wronged by many people. I just move on. I have to forgive and move on. God is right that forgiveness makes everything better. And it's something [I've] taught my children, and they do the same. And my parents are that way as well. You know, I see people who live with faith and I see people who live without, and those who live with faith have a much better road, a much happier life."

Being involved in a miraculous rescue, as he was, stirred up a lot of feelings and reflections for Eric. He believes that God was reaching out to him not just to rescue those teens but to remind him of his need to remain faithful, "At times everybody, you know, loses sight of faith or just isn't as focused on it. And I do believe that God's intervention did renew my faith. It sparked conversations with my family, with my friends about faith. And for months and months afterwards, we had very healthy conversations about faith and about religion with my brothers, my sister, with my nieces and nephews, with so many people. A lot of my friends confided in me who I didn't even know were faithful, who I didn't even know were religious people, that they said a lot of prayers themselves after hearing about what I experienced. So it absolutely was a kick in the tail for me to be reminded of who's in charge. And you know, that reminds me to stay strong in faith, regardless of the trials and tribulations."

Eric faced difficulties in both his personal and professional lives, and he did lose sight of God at times. But it wasn't only in the darker times that happened. As he explained, "Sometimes you forget the reason for your success. You can easily enjoy the pleasures of life as if you did it yourself. You take credit for all the things going so well. This miracle rescue reminded me that the reason things are going so well is in part because I'm faithful. I rely on times of prayer. I rely on meditation. I rely on leaving things to God and knowing things are out of my hands. And that takes away a lot of stress and relieves a lot of anxiety and allows me to focus on things that are much more important. And it's easy to forget about that message. It's easy to walk away from that for a while. And something like this certainly puts you back in the right track."

Though Eric didn't say so, I was struck by several thoughts. One was the way the *Amen* had arrived just in time. So many things had gone wrong before and during the early stages of Eric's voyage that only God could make them right. Even the smallest of delays had contributed not only to Eric's rising frustration but also to the miraculous intervention of which he was a small part. It's a good reminder of how we never know what part we're playing in the enormous machinery that is God's design and craftsmanship.

In addition, as Eric pointed out, not only do we all lose sight of God, but the noise and interference of our daily lives frequently result in our not being able to hear Him calling out to us. Unlike the *Amen* and its crew, which could have easily, but gratefully and miraculously did not, cruise past the shouting teenagers, God will always persist in His efforts to reach us. That day on the Atlantic, not only did God listen for, hear, and respond to Heather and Tyler's request, He called to Eric and his friends.

We are in a constant dialogue with the Lord our God, and as we sometimes do in life, we may drift into and out of full awareness of what is being said to us and its importance. God not only saved Tyler and Heather that day but had a powerful influence on the life of Eric and his family and friends. His message was carried on the wind and the water, moving far beyond who we might have believed His Word was intended for, to all of us.

One thing that Jesus' disciples forgot, on the water, was that God is always in control. What they didn't realize, of course, was that God was in the boat with them. It can be so easy to focus on the storms of life—the things right in front of us—and to forget that taking a nap in the hold of our ship is the Son of God.

WHEN YOUR MIND SAYS "JUMP"

A desperate act sets a mother on the road to healing.

> The LORD himself goes before you and will be
> with you; he will never leave you nor forsake you.
> Do not be afraid; do not be discouraged.
> —DEUTERONOMY 31:8

Joseph couldn't remember how long he'd been underground. Every day the routines of life in jail were the same. For a while, he had kept time by tracing the bars of light crossing the ceiling of the prison. After a year, he abandoned even that.

Joseph had grown up in the wide-open country. At night in his cell, his dreams were full of stars, cattle, open fields, visions of that childhood—before his family had forgotten their youngest brother.

Other prisoners came and went. They said they'd remember him, but they didn't.

Forgotten. Alone. Everyone seemed to forget Joseph eventually.

God, Joseph prayed, where are you?

Joseph was imprisoned in the kingdom of Egypt. He would later become one of the twelve fathers of the nation of Israel. But in that hole in the ground, he must have felt that he'd never be anyone's father.

We know the technicolor coat part, but Joseph's story contained many moments when, from his perspective, he was alone, forgotten, hopeless.

But he wasn't. Not really.

DEPRESSION FEELS A BIT LIKE that: falling into a hole with no way out. Wisconsin mom Tina Zahn had struggled with depression for much of her life, but postpartum depression still threw her into a tailspin. Even thinking of her favorite Bible story, the story of Joseph, didn't help bring her out of it. It felt as though she couldn't hear God's voice.

The silence would lead her to do something that no one, she included, could really understand. Something desperate.

All because she felt alone.

"Why can't you snap out of this?" The words, spoken by a relative, seemed to come to her from a million miles away. Tina was living at her mother's house then, recovering from the birth of her son. She had spent her days staring dully into the middle distance, wondering why she couldn't feel something—anything.

But with those words, she suddenly felt everything all at once.

Years of pain pressed into that moment: Tina's lifelong depression; her difficult childhood; her first and most basic instinct that the solution to her problems was to withdraw, to push everyone around her away.

She had just one thought: run.

So she did.

She leapt to her feet and flew out of the room, grabbing the car keys on her way out. Nothing got through to her, not her mother's appeal that she turn around, not her six-year-old daughter's plaintive plea as she stood in the driveway. She climbed into the family car and sped off down the road from Shawano to Green Bay, Wisconsin.

Tina refused to listen. She heard just one voice. The one that urged her to go the highest bridge in the area and jump. Pressing the gas pedal flat to the floor of the car, she flew down the road, weaving with deadly certainty through traffic. The miles sped by in minutes. When she came to the bridge she stepped out of the car and strode with purpose toward the edge.

She clambered over the concrete barrier. It slowed her for just a moment. Below lay the dull blue surface of the Fox River, a two-hundred-foot drop.

She jumped.

For a millisecond she hung in the air, a moment she can no longer remember.

And then, out of nowhere, a hand grabbed her arm.

ONE OF SCRIPTURE'S MOST CONSISTENT promises is: do not fear; God is with you. But it's never easy to remember that everlasting truth when we're in a hole. Tina Zahn knew what that was like. A whole lifetime had led her to a moment when she decided to turn her back on everything. But if you had looked at her life just a few years before the jump, it would have seemed—from the outside— like the American Dream fulfilled.

Tina and her husband, Daniel, were living the good life. He

had a successful career as a mechanical engineer. She was thriving as a top-earning pharmaceutical representative. They lived in a custom-built showcase home of the kind they had always dreamed of owning. Their lives were enriched when they welcomed their daughter, Sarah, into the world in 1998.

Yet underneath it all, Tina's mental health was fragile. She was particularly susceptive to depression, having spent years fighting through it. Even when surrounded by people, she felt isolated. "You can be an extrovert," she said. "That doesn't mean you don't feel lonely."

She had felt alone many times in her life, going back to a childhood when she was abused. In time, with the assistance of a counselor, she had begun to recover from that experience. The counseling stopped. She and her therapist applied a small Band-Aid to a large wound and tacitly agreed to move on.

Tina became depressed again but didn't seek counseling. Withdrawal and isolation were the "cure." She'd emerge from the dark place, squint against the bright lights for a moment, and go back to pretending that everything was normal. From that experience, a pattern was born: suffer in silence, build a facade of happiness, don't tell anyone about your or your family's dark history.

The problem was that Tina's "normal," as for most of us, was a cycle of ups and downs. In 2000, the up cycle in her professional life turned downward. The pharmaceutical giant she worked for experienced a downturn of its own, and five hundred people across the country lost their jobs. Tina was among that number. She was stunned and angry. Without warning, after giving her all to that company, this was what she was being given in return?

She'd done the right thing. She'd worked when she was

depressed. She'd sacrificed spending time with her child and husband while on the road doing sales calls. She'd never called in sick.

Shortly after the phone call during which she was let go (she was too numb to register disbelief that the "breakup" was done over the phone!), she stood in the kitchen of their home with her mind and spirit roiling, stung by the company's ingratitude.

She looked out the window and watched the wind whip the tree branches like the tides rushing in and out. Above that the expanse of sky was a clean sheet. Instead of the vibrant greens and blues she knew she should have been viewing, the scene was rendered in tones of gray.

"I asked the Lord, 'What's next?'" she said.

What followed startled her. She wasn't expecting an answer. But she got one.

"I heard a voice inside me say, 'You know that building that looks like an insurance company down the street? I need you to go to that church.'"

Tina had been raised going to traditional Catholic and later to Lutheran churches. She was a regular churchgoer into adulthood. Eventually, she began attending where husband Daniel's parents worshipped. God was always a part of her life, prayer a common practice. But He was on the periphery, a presence outside her main field of vision, like the neighbor's swing set and playhouse she knew was past the edge of the window but could not see.

If she was looking for a sign from God that day, she got one. If she was looking for a sign from the church announcing its presence, she wouldn't find it. This non-denominational church was housed, almost hidden, in a multipurpose office building. She had passed the site frequently but hadn't realized that it was a church.

She thought more about what God had said. At first she thought that she didn't need another church. She had one. But the more she considered, the more she realized that her current spiritual life felt more like a duty than a desire. She'd show up on a Sunday, nod and smile perfunctorily at the other members of the congregation, slide into a pew and gaze up at the stained glass, and say the prayers and responses that came to her reflexively.

She had also become conscious that even now that her depression had eased a bit, there was a great void in her life. She couldn't seem to fill that gap on her own.

That Sunday, accompanied by her sister, Tina walked up to the doors of the space that Green Bay Community Church occupied in the office building. She was immediately struck by the welcoming group that congregated at the entrance.

At first she thought that maybe it was novelty that drew her in—people were holding cups of coffee from the shop inside—but the timbre of the people and the place captivated her. She said, "I just thought, when I had gone through the first service, 'This is where I belong.'" When the pastor began the prayer that invited people to welcome the Lord into their lives, Tina prayed with a fervor and a feeling she'd never experienced before.

She'd found what she'd been looking for, even if there was no sign outside the building announcing its presence. Like God, though, the spirit of that community was everywhere and in everyone. She had just needed a nudge to dislodge the scales from her eyes.

But while what I would call a "God-shaped hole" in her life had been filled, she still had struggles ahead. Depression has a way of hanging on to us.

Following the birth of her second child in the late spring of 2004, Tina was hit by postpartum depression. She retreated inward. She felt like a bug, curling up tightly inside a hard shell that shielded her from elements that threatened her: guilt, anxiety, the suffocating effects of her sadness. The "cure" was nearly as bad as the disease. The drugs prescribed for her numbed her mentally and physically.

One of the biggest lies that depression tells us is that we're totally alone. During Tina's recovery, her friends from church, her mother, her in-laws, and her husband all rushed to help, but she was barely aware of what was happening around her. The women from church took turns coming to the house to cook and clean. Her in-laws watched over Sarah and little baby Noah.

Unable to care for herself, Tina moved in with her mother. Tina's mom made sure that her daughter got out of the house, taking her on visits to friends in Shawano. Amid all the movement, Tina felt increasingly isolated. She was nearly comatose both at home and in the homes of others. She sat staring, lost in nonthought, as if she were in a crowded airport terminal as people and conversations sped past her on a moving walkway.

Tina knew about postpartum depression. What she didn't know was that it often gets worse with each successive child. She'd had it with her first child, but it was even greater with her second. Postpartum depression hits a peak three months after a birth. That was when she snapped completely. It was the day she decided to jump.

That day, July 19, 2004, Tina listened to depression's great lie and took it to heart. She was determined to cut herself off from everyone in her life, forever. She was determined to be alone.

But she wasn't. Her family and community weren't about to let her withdraw beyond rescue. They stepped up in miraculous ways.

TINA'S MOM TOOK ACTION.

As Tina was bolting out of the house, Tina's mom heard her ranting about her destination: the bridge. Unable to prevent her daughter's flight, her mother leapt for the phone and immediately called her son-in-law, Daniel. He in turn dialed 911, describing what was happening and then rushed out to his own car.

By the time Tina reached the highway, her husband was already heading in the direction of the residence in Shawano. The two passed each other, and Daniel U-turned on the median and took off in pursuit of his wife.

Meanwhile, state trooper Les Boldt had just ended his shift and was sitting at the post office filling out his time card preparing to mail it. When he returned to his car, he turned on his radio and heard the call about a high-speed vehicle on the highway leading to Leo Frigo Memorial Bridge. Boldt immediately joined a chase that would reach 105 miles per hour.

Boldt was a veteran officer trained in how to handle suicidal "jumpers" and must have known that this situation would take a high level of risk on his part. He was all in. He was right behind Tina when she pulled over at the apex of the bridge. As she got out of the car and deliberately marched toward the edge of the bridge, he was just emerging from his cruiser. He called out to her, "Ma'am! Ma'am!"

She paid no attention.

Boldt saw in an instant what was about to happen, and knew he had only seconds to act. He dashed after her and grabbed her wrist an instant before she was beyond saving.

Video from the patrol car's dash-mounted camera captured the harrowing scene. Boldt's last-minute catch left him leaning over the brink. When Tina had jumped, her feet had caught on a lip of pavement that stuck out a few inches beyond the concrete barrier, just enough to arrest her momentum for a second. In that second, Trooper Boldt managed to drag Tina back. She fought him, jerking backward. He held on, bracing himself against the barrier.

"I wanted to fall," she remembered. "He would not let that happen."

If it had not been for that concrete barrier, which Boldt used as leverage to pull Tina back, it is doubtful that he would have been able to hold on for the sixteen seconds before a fellow officer grabbed Tina's other arm. A third officer arrived on the scene and grabbed her legs. They pulled her back over the barrier to safety.

A lot of things had to go right for that successful outcome to come about. Tina owes much to Officer Boldt's brave refusal to follow procedures that would have kept him safe but allowed her to fall to her death. However, she firmly believes that it was the intervention of her church friends, who prayed regularly for her, that enabled the just-in-time rescue attempt to succeed. At each turn it is possible to see the hand of God in action, invoked by the prayers of Tina's family and her church.

After the jump, many things in Tina's life changed. Though her road to recovery was long and arduous, she has come out on the other side of the experience a stronger woman and a stronger believer. But, as I said earlier, depression hangs on. After being rescued, Tina was offered electroconvulsive therapy (ECT) treatments to thwart her depressive episodes. As a result, she lost a lot of memories. That's a common side effect that some are willing to live with. (ECT treatments are considered a treatment of last resort for suicidal and self-harming patients. They do work more quickly and with a higher rate of success than antidepressant drugs, according to data from Johns Hopkins, but the effects are short term.)[4]

Though Tina has no recollection of returning to church, in the intervening years, her faith community welcomed her back with open arms. In fact, something happened that you wouldn't expect.

Tina found that people kept coming up to her for support. "They would . . . share their depression stories, their suicidal thoughts. They thought they were alone. But after meeting me, they would say they found someone who felt the same way that they did."

Prayer is a mainstay for her. Her prayer life begins with a morning daily devotional with Scripture and ends in the evening with a prayer session in the hot tub. People frequently come to her to ask for her help with prayers of intercession. She is now a published author, an advocate for openness and education about mental health issues, such as postpartum depression, and a devoted mother and church leader.

One of Tina's favorite Bible stories is that of Joseph, the favored son who was sold into slavery by his jealous brothers. Despite the suffering he experienced as a slave in Egypt, he eventually rose to be a mighty ruler in the land. That status ultimately allowed him to save his family when their food supply was devastated by a famine. The story appeals to Tina because she feels a deep connection to Joseph's desire to do the right thing, to endure in his faith despite the difficulties he faced.

At the end of Joseph's story in the Book of Genesis, he doesn't pretend that his suffering was easy or light. But he does highlight the good that has come out of his exile. He tells his brothers, "You intended to harm me, but God intended for good to accomplish what is now being done, the saving of many lives. So then, don't be afraid." (Genesis 50:20–21)

Today, Tina says that her experience on the bridge has meant her world expanded in unforeseen ways. "God opened it up so that I could share my life so that others could get some hope from it." Reflecting on Joseph's words, she offered this advice: "Everything we encounter can be used for good, but not everything we encounter is God."

There have been many points in Tina's life when depression convinced her that no one was strong enough to catch her. But the force of God's intervening love was so great that He pulled Tina into His safe embrace. Tina has felt the presence of the Lord's safety on her path of healing from that day forward.

THE STRENGTH OF A PRAYER CLOSET

A grandmother's astonishing prayer inspires the world.

> Then they cried out to the LORD in their trouble,
> and he brought them out of their distress.
> He stilled the storm to a whisper.
>
> —PSALM 107:28–29

Earnestine Reese's home was gone. Brick by brick, the tornado had demolished the structure, leaving behind no walls, no ceiling—nothing but wind-torn pieces. Now, beneath a troubled but silent sky, the family surveyed what remained. And amid the shredded cabinets, waterlogged couches, and chunks of brick wall, seventy-two-year-old Earnestine praised the Lord.

Seated on rubble, the grandmother told her grandson over video chat, "Tell God thank you! Hey! So glad. Nothing but the power of God."

Alight with the grace of the Holy Spirit, Earnestine was laughing.

On March 3, 2019, a series of severe storms, spawning tornadoes, ravaged a portion of the American South from Florida to Georgia to Alabama. Twenty-three people lost their lives, all of them from Lee County, Alabama. Twisters leveled homes and businesses, uprooted trees, and caused millions of dollars in damage. But the punishing weather did not lay a glove on the heart, spirit, and faith of Lee County or the rest of the region affected by the violent weather. Earnestine's story came to symbolize the courage and the belief in God that helped people sustain their faith that they would come back from tragedy.

A resident of Beauregard in Lee County, Earnestine broke her hip when her house was destroyed, but in a viral YouTube video shared in the immediate aftermath of the storm, she was shown seated on the site where her home had once stood, thanking God for her family's preservation.

Wrapped in a green football jersey with the number two emblazoned it, a tube feeding her life-sustaining oxygen, Earnestine proclaimed, "I thank the Lord!" Later she instructed, "You hear me. Tell God thank you." She laughed and repeated, "Tell God thank you." As the camera, held by Earnestine's nephew, panned around, it showed the path of destruction, denuded trees, an overturned water heater, a couch, portions of the roof, sections of fallen brick wall. Yet in the background Earnestine cried out in praise of the lifesaving power of God and not the destructive power of the storm. She praised the Lord, directly crediting His intervention for the saving of her family's life.

The drama had begun the day before. Earnestine's daughter, LaShawn Wilson, and LaShawn's husband, Kolaya, lived next door. In an account she later gave to AL.com, LaShawn explained how when she had first heard the severe weather warnings, she, her husband, and their son, Qumran—named for the location in which the Dead Sea Scrolls were discovered—ran to Earnestine's aid.

They helped the seventy-two-year-old get into the bathroom, the room they deemed the safest in the house. And then they waited. Earnestine instructed her grandson to ask the Savior for help. LaShawn asked him to pray several times.[5]

People have frequently described the roar of a tornado as being like that of a freight train passing nearby. It's difficult to imagine how frightening it must be to be in a house where the roof is torn off and the walls collapse. From inside the house, the shrieking sound of nails being pulled out, bricks tumbling to the ground, glass smashing, and objects being turned into projectiles must have been terrifying.

Remarkably, the inhabitants of the house came out of the maelstrom alive. After the storm passed, they looked around. Nearly every bit of the house frame had collapsed. Only one small section still stood. They were amazed, but likely not surprised, to see that the prayer closet that Earnestine had used as a sanctuary and the site of her conversations with God was the only thing left standing. Every other structural element of the house had been torn asunder, but that sacred space, which Earnestine had used for decades to communicate and commune with God stood strong.

"I believe that was a way for everybody to see that you pray and you believe God and he will never leave you nor forsake you," Earnestine said.[6]

Even in the midst of the storm and the house collapsing around them, LaShawn felt the presence of God. Even the collapse of the structure itself felt providential. "This presence, I describe it as the hand of God, was holding us down," she told AL.com.[7] She saw being pinned down by the wreckage to have been a saving grace.

With winds that powerful, their bodies could easily have been picked up and carried away. Their injuries could have been much worse. They could easily have been killed, yet their lives had been saved. When what felt like a second wave of the series of storms came through, LaShawn clung to the bathroom's vanity as the cold wind and rain pelted her.

In the meantime, neighbors, some of whom were relatives, rushed over to help free Earnestine. Heedless of their own needs, they offered aid. Earnestine was still trapped beneath the rubble, and they worked to free her.[8]

It's hard to imagine what Earnestine experienced, but it's a beautiful testament to her faith and the power of prayer that she and her family were able to praise God in the immediate aftermath of such devastation. Two tornados blew through the area, one estimated to be a half-mile wide with winds between 136 and 165 miles per hour.

It wasn't the first time Alabama had been struck by deadly tornados. In a series of storms in 2011, more than sixty tornados had touched down and more than 230 Alabamans had lost their lives. Lee County is located in what many have nicknamed "Dixie Alley," the southern states where severe weather strikes are frequent and residents eye the skies warily. Alabama also, according to a Pew Research Center demographic study, has the highest percentage of Evangelical Christians in the country.[9] But numbers rarely tell the full story. It's the testimony of men and women such as Earnestine Reese and many others who have lived through horrifying experiences that truly testifies to the faith of Alabamans. She survived the storm, and her praise fired the imagination and passionate faith of others around the country.

It isn't merely a close-knit community, it's a place where kinship ties are strong, lasting, and continually present. The twenty-three individuals who died all resided in a one-square-mile area. Seven of the twenty-three were related to Earnestine and her family.[10] Their neighborhood is also a place where faith and worship are woven into the fabric of everyday life. Local businesses gave money and cars to people who'd lost everything in the tragedy. People on the internet poured donations into GoFundMe appeals. Community members pulled together and sought solace and hope together. They needed to; in addition to the twenty-three fatalities, ninety more people were injured.

In an interview a year later, Earnestine said, "You can't help but to not think about [the storm]. It'll never be the same."[11]

In the immediate aftermath of the storm, local people rushed to churches, many bringing relief supplies. Later, when the extent of Earnestine's injuries and her needs were known, neighbors worked together to help her out. A medical center's foundation provided her with an apartment while she underwent rehabilitation. An area Baptist church helped furnish it for her. Earnestine wasn't the only one who received aid and care. Fifty miles from the tornados, in Georgia, a grandmother named Heidy McConnell discovered a fragment of one of LaShawn's family photos and returned it. "I know if it was me, and I lost all my pictures, I would take back whatever I could," Heidy said.

"That's one picture . . . but it's mine, it's me. It's a piece that I lost," LaShawn said. "To know I still have something. It may seem like nothing, but it's something."[12]

As we've seen countless times in the face of a tragedy, people pull together. They rebuild their homes and businesses. They mourn the lives lost and dedicate themselves to their memory. They don't forget. Some maintain their faith. Some strengthen it.

Many did what they could to repair the damage. By the end of December 2019, Earnestine had moved into a new home. Reverend Franklin Graham, with Samaritan's Purse, had heard of Earnestine's plight and the remarkable story of her prayer closet. He made it the organization's goal to build a new residence for the woman who had inspired so many with her message of faith and gratitude.

In a Facebook live interview with WRBL out of Columbus, Georgia, Earnestine said, "What a blessing. . . . Oh, honey, this is the greatest present. I couldn't think of no other present I would want, but to have y'all here with us and [the new house] I'm seeing. And seeing how good God has been."[13]

Prayer was deeply worked into the history of Earnestine's family. In a later interview with AL.com, LaShawn said, "That's what we do. That's how we get through. That's what's getting us through even now."[14]

LaShawn had likely relied on prayers for the prior three years when she was taking care of her mother while living next door. Complications after a surgical procedure made it difficult for Earnestine to care for herself. When Earnestine met Franklin Graham, she told him how she had admired and prayed with his father, Billy, on TV. "Well, your faith has been a blessing to us," Graham said. "And your family's faith has been a blessing."

Earnestine replied, "That's all we have. We grew up with it and we know about Jesus. And we have been witnessing a long time." Aware of the cameras, she joked that she was happy that their meeting was going to be on TV. "Let's talk about Jesus!" she said, clasping Graham's hand.[15]

Countless stories of a Samaritan's grace go untold every day. From allowing someone with fewer items to move ahead in the checkout line to writing a large donation check, no matter the size of the gesture, when such acts of faith inspire others to similar actions, the wounds of the larger world can be healed and millions can be helped.

Christ's cross stands as a symbolic reminder of the sacrifice he made for all of us. Earnestine's prayer closet became a symbol for many people of the power of prayer. Others considered it a miracle. Regardless, the message is much the same: survive and move on. God will always be there, especially in the darkest of hours, when it seems impossible that our voices can be heard above the chaos. God is truly great. Amid the loss of life and great personal tragedy, millions of people were inspired, and His message of hope, sacrifice, and service shines through.

LaShawn emphasized the importance of prayer but, she pointed out, it didn't have to be in a closet. "It's finding a place you can tap into that moment with God."[16]

Earnestine's prayer closet is a reminder that we can connect with God any time and any place. He is always accessible to us. It doesn't take a deadly storm or a miraculous moment of survival for Him to be active in our lives. That is the miracle of our relationship with our Lord and Savior Jesus Christ. In life's dramatic moments and at the most mundane of times, such as when hanging a dress on a hanger in a closet, He is here, and through our faith in Him, all things are possible.

Earnestine's gratitude and faith are astonishing in their purity. How many of us could lose everything and still praise God? It is important not to minimize the sense of loss and irreparable harm that occurs when a home is wiped away, but Earnestine's praise truly does remind us of Jesus' words of wisdom: "Do not store up for yourselves treasures on earth, where moth and vermin destroy, and where thieves break in and steal. But store up for yourselves treasures in heaven, where moths and vermin do not destroy, and where thieves do not break in and steal. For where your treasure is, there your heart will be also." (Matthew 6:19–21)

Earnestine passed away on January 24, 2022. This is for certain: her treasure in Heaven must surely be great.

THE PRAYER ORDERED BY A GENERAL

How a simple prayer turned the tide of World War II.

> "Should you not fear me?" declares the LORD.
> "Should you not tremble in my presence? I made
> the sand a boundary for the sea, an everlasting
> barrier it cannot cross. The waves may roll, but
> they cannot prevail; they may roar, but they cannot
> cross it."
>
> —JEREMIAH 5:22

As dawn turned to morning on December 8, 1944, Chaplain James H. O'Neill sat in his office preparing for the day. As the chief chaplain of General George S. Patton, Jr.'s Third Army, O'Neill was with the troops that had made their headquarters in Caserne Molifor in Nancy, France.[17]

Chaplain O'Neill had been with General Patton throughout all of his campaigns of the war so far, and he had great respect for his commanding officer. When the phone rang, O'Neill picked it up immediately.

"This is General Patton," he heard from the other end of the line. "Do you have a good prayer for weather? We must do something about those rains if we are to win the war."

O'Neill looked out the window at the steady downpour that had plagued Patton's tanks and infantrymen throughout the Moselle and Saar campaigns since September. It was tough to push the front farther toward Germany under the constant deluges. For now, the Allied forces had dug in and were protecting France from another German advance toward Paris. But beyond that, the war seemed as though it would be at a stalemate until the weather improved.

The chaplain immediately surmised why Patton was asking. "I will check, sir, and let you know within the hour."

O'Neill quickly searched through the few prayer books he had on hand and found nothing fitting. As the hour drained away, he decided there was nothing to do but write something himself. At his typewriter, he composed the following prayer on a three-by-five-inch file card:

> Almighty and most merciful Father, we humbly beseech Thee, of Thy great goodness, to restrain these immoderate rains with which we have had to contend. Grant us fair weather for Battle. Graciously hearken to us as soldiers who call upon Thee that, armed with Thy power, we may advance from victory to victory, and crush the oppression and wickedness of our enemies and establish Thy justice among men and nations. Amen.

When he finished typing, he looked at the card and reviewed the words again. It seemed unlikely that the general wanted it for his private devotional time; more likely it was to reprint and pass among the troops. With Christmas just a few weeks away, he flipped the card over and typed a Christmas greeting with a place for the general to sign.

Finally, he pulled the card from the typewriter, donned his heavy trench coat, and crossed the courtyard of the old French military barracks to present the card to the general himself.

Upon arrival, General Patton ushered the chaplain in, took and read the prayer, nodded, and handed it back.

He then issued an order: "Have 250,000 copies printed and see to it that every man in the Third Army gets one."

"Very well, Sir!" the chaplain replied, a little surprised by the enormity of the task he had just been given. "But here if you might, sir," he responded, showing the general the Christmas greeting on the other side of the card.

The general took it again and read. He smiled at the initiative. "Very good," he said.

"If the General would sign the card, it would add a personal touch that I am sure the men would like."

The general crossed to his desk, signed it, and held it back out to the chaplain. Not rising from his desk, he said, "Chaplain, sit down for a moment; I want to talk to you about this business of prayer."

As the chaplain sat, the general rubbed his face and remained silent for a moment. Then he rose to his full six-foot-two-inch height and crossed to the window. His uniform was crisply starched and with every detail in proper place. He was in top physical condition, and his bearing betrayed his years of disciplined living as a soldier. Looking at the angry weather, he asked, "Chaplain, how much praying is being done in the Third Army?"

"Does the general mean by chaplains, or by the men?"

"By everybody," he replied.

Thinking for a moment, the chaplain responded, "I am afraid to admit it, but I do not believe that much praying is going on. When there is fighting, everyone prays, but now with this constant rain—when things are quiet, dangerously quiet—men just sit and wait for things to happen. Prayer out here is difficult. Both chaplains and men are removed from a special building with a steeple. Prayer to most of them is a formal, ritualized affair, involving special posture and a liturgical setting. I do not believe that much praying is being done."

The general crossed back to his desk, sat down, picked up a pencil between his two index fingers, and leaned back.

"Chaplain, I am a strong believer in prayer," he said. "There are three ways that men get what they want: by planning, by working, and by praying. Any great military operation takes careful planning, or thinking. Then you must have well-trained troops to carry it out: that's working. But between the plan and the operation there is always an unknown. That unknown spells defeat or victory, success or failure. It is the reaction of the actors to the ordeal when it actually comes. Some people call that getting the breaks; I call it God. God has His part, or margin, in everything. That's where prayer comes in."

He paused for a moment and then continued, "Up to now, in the Third Army, God has been very good to us. We have never retreated; we have suffered no defeats, no famine, no epidemics. This is because a lot of people back home are praying for us. We were lucky in Africa, in Sicily, and in Italy, simply because people prayed. But we have to pray for ourselves, too. A good soldier is not made merely by making him think and work. There is something in every soldier that goes deeper than thinking or working—it's his 'guts.' It is something that he has built in there: it is a world of truth and power that is higher than himself. Great living is not all output of thought and work. A man has to have intake as well. I don't know what you call it, but I call it Religion, Prayer, or God."

He talked briefly about Gideon's fight in the Bible, where prayer had been critical, and men the general had known depended on prayer as if it were their very lifeline. He spoke eloquently, and the chaplain hung on every word. Then the general concluded, "We must ask God to stop these rains. These rains are that margin that holds defeat or victory. If we all pray . . . it will be like plugging in on a current whose source is in Heaven. I believe that prayer completes that circuit. It is power."

With those words, the general rose from his desk a second time, and the chaplain did as well, knowing that was the sign that their conversation had ended. O'Neill returned to his field desk and, still under the inspiration of the general's words, typed out what became known as Training Letter No. 5.

In it, he wrote about the importance of prayer and touched on many of the points the general had made in their discussion. When the general read it, he approved it to be distributed without any changes. Then, under the chief chaplain's direction, the 250,000 prayer cards and training letters were printed and distributed to the troops and 486 chaplains of the Third Army. The material was disseminated from December 11 and 12, which proved to be providential timing.

Throughout that time, the weather remained miserable and grew colder, as was normal for that time of year in the northern forests of France and the Ardennes region of Belgium. Taking that into account, on December 16, Hitler's armies made their last great push for victory under the cover of heavy fog, which limited visibility to a few yards, and pounding rain, which muffled the sound of their tanks.

With much of the mud now frozen in the harshest weather of the year, the German Sixth Panzer Army began making lightning-fast surprise attacks along the eighty-eight-mile front that was tenuously held by the Allied forces. On December 19, Patton's Third Army tank divisions turned north to try to meet the German offensive under the continued bad weather and almost immediately stalled.

The famous Battle of the Bulge had begun.

The initial German push caused chaos for the Allied forces. Rumors quickly spread of defeats and massacred troops and civilians. Fearing the worst, Belgians began taking down their Allied flags and putting up swastikas, hoping to find favor with the Germans when they inevitably retook the region. The temperature plummeted. Over the six weeks of the battle, the average temperature was 20 degrees F. with about eight inches of snow on the ground.[18]

As the Germans wreaked havoc almost without opposition, they quickly surrounded the strategic village of Bastogne, which was the base of some 12,000 Allied troops, including the famed 101st Airborne Division, the "Screaming Eagles." Outnumbering the Allied troops five to one, the Germans demanded surrender. Brigadier General Anthony McAuliffe, the commander of the division, responded to the demand with one word: *"Nuts!"* Despite that resolve, however, things looked hopeless as the rains poured on.

The air support needed was grounded due to the weather, and Patton and his tanks were unable to make a coordinated counterstrike. He needed at least a twenty-four-hour break in the rains to mobilize his troops. When he heard McAuliffe's response, he was more determined than ever to rescue him, saying "A man that eloquent has to be saved."[19]

Then, on Christmas morning, the weather broke. The rains stopped and the fog dissipated, to the great surprise of US forecasters, who had seen no indicators of anything but more bad weather ahead. For most of the next week, there were bright, clear skies and perfect flying weather. The day after Christmas, Patton's forces, supported by a continuous flow of thousands of Allied aircraft, moved the Third Army into position, broke the German lines, and rescued McAuliffe and his soldiers in the Bastogne.

More miraculously, the fair weather continued with only a few breaks. What followed was the fiercest fighting and heaviest casualties of World War II. According to the US Department of Defense, more than a million Allied troops, including roughly half a million Americans, fought in the Battle of the Bulge. Approximately 19,000 soldiers were killed, 47,500 were wounded, and more than 23,000 went missing in action. On the other side, close to 100,000 Germans were killed, wounded, or captured.[20]

The heavy fighting continued for another month, and the Allies declared the battle over on January 25, 1945. The German troops had withdrawn. The Allies then regrouped and pushed on toward Berlin. Less than five months later, the war in Europe ended when the Nazis surrendered on May 7.

"The Ardennes campaign of 1944–45 was only one in a series of difficult engagements in the battle for Europe," John S. D. Eisenhower wrote in *The Bitter Woods: The Battle of the Bulge*. "Nevertheless, it can be said that the Ardennes campaign epitomized them all. For it was here that American and German combat soldiers met in the decisive struggle that broke the back of the Nazi war machine."[21]

One of the interesting and complicated things about Patton was his relationship with religion. Practical by nature, he was willing to use whatever worked to achieve his goal. But he also had eccentric though rock-solid beliefs in things such as reincarnation (he was convinced that he'd lived many previous lives, all of them as soldiers).

Through my research for this book, I've gotten to know many amazing believers. I actually first met Benjamin Patton, the general's grandson, a few years back. I reached out since then, to talk about the faith walk of the general who had led so many at such an important time in America's history. Benjamin told me that his grandfather "really looked to the clouds for" solutions to his problems, but he didn't proselytize about what was in those clouds.

"My grandfather's faith is hard to codify," Benjamin explained. "It was deep but different than what most would think. His beliefs were utilitarian. . . . Always on a mission to complete a task or win a battle, my grandfather was focused on finding the right prayer, the right word to one end—the support needed for things to work out well."[22]

Patton's intensity and laser focus on the mission supported by keeping the Lord's word as gospel has lived on. Benjamin calls it a legacy of faith. He told me, "My own dad, Major General George Patton, took it further, often quoting from Ecclesiastes: 'Whatsoever your hand finds to do, do it with all your might.'" (Ecclesiastes 9:10)

He added, "That was his big lesson to me. You know, live in the present. Whatever battle you're facing, fight it."

In late January 1945, just days after the Allied victory was declared, Chaplain O'Neill and General Patton met again in Luxembourg. Seeing the chaplain, the general walked straight up to him and smiled. "Well, Padre, our prayers worked. I knew they would."

Then Patton took his riding crop and cracked O'Neill on the side of his steel helmet, which Chief Chaplain O'Neill knew was Patton's way of saying, "Well done."[23]

God helps us see beyond what's possible. His gift of imagination and innovation removes the scales from our eyes, unveiling new possibilities beyond our wildest dreams.

Purpose

"With man this is impossible, but with God all things are possible."

—MATTHEW 19:26

WANT A JOB DONE RIGHT?
CALL A MOM

When doctors couldn't ease the pain of Sarah's son with
spina bifida, she prayed for help—and God gave her a
dream that changed the world.

> May the favor of the LORD our God rest on us;
> establish the work of our hands for us—yes,
> establish the work of our hands.
>
> —PSALM 90:17

*L*ook, Sarah," Dr. David Vandersteen said to the distraught
mother sitting on the other side of his desk. "This is our only
option."

Sarah Olson didn't flinch. "There has to be another way," she
insisted. "Levi suffered for months with complications, infections,
surgeries—and he was in so much pain. You know he was passing
out from the pain, right?"

"I know. Some people, like your son, experience overwhelming pain," the pediatric urologist said with compassion. "But we've looked at all the options, and nothing else is going to work for him."

Four years earlier, in 2016, Sarah's son Levi had been born with spina bifida, undergoing more than a half-dozen surgeries in the first years of his life. When Levi was just three years old, surgeons created an opening called a stoma in his abdomen to provide a way for his bladder to drain without invasive catheterization through the urethra. To keep the stoma open while it healed, they inserted a temporary catheter through the newly formed opening and into the bladder. Hopefully, within a month, the temporary catheter would no longer be needed.

Though the stoma surgery had gone perfectly, the catheter proved to be a nightmare for Levi, causing recurring infections, excruciating bladder spasms, and additional surgeries. And because of all the complications, the stoma hadn't been healing well, so there seemed to be no relief in sight. Remember Levi was just a toddler.

After six unbearable months, Sarah demanded that doctors give Levi a break. They removed the catheter and allowed the stoma to close, but with this warning: "Eventually we will need to try this again."

"Eventually" arrived far too soon.

Sarah knew that Levi, now four years old, needed the stoma. And Dr. Vandersteen, practicing at the Minneapolis Children's Hospital, was one of the best pediatric urologists in the nation.

"All right, we'll do this," she conceded during the consultation in his office. "But we're not using the Foley catheter again. I'm not going to kill my kid with a catheter. There's got to be another solution."

"I don't know what to tell you, Sarah," the doctor said gently.

"I've been doing this a long time. I wish there were something else, but this is the best option we have for this condition. Nothing else exists. If you want something different, you would have to invent it yourself."

As Sarah left the office, she had a single thought: If saving my son means inventing a medical device, okay, then. I guess this mama is going to invent something!

The first thing she did was go home and start praying. Raised in a Christian family, she had believed in Jesus from the time she was four years old and talking to God had always been an important part of her life.

She admitted that when she started praying, she was angry. "I was throwing a temper tantrum with the Lord," she recalled. "I told him, 'Look, I'm not okay with this solution. It seems this catheter works for other people, but it's not working for Levi. Why is this happening to my little boy? And if you love him more than I love him, why are you allowing this?'"

Outside her bedroom door, she heard her three children—Zakary, Levi, and Tilly—playing. "Lord," she continued praying, her heart softer now, "the doctor just said I had to invent something. And I don't even know what that means."

A college dropout, Sarah had no training in engineering, the medical field, or the development of new devices—not anything close to those subjects.

Her prayer continued: "What am I supposed to do, Lord? Invent something? I think I'm a good mom, but I wouldn't have the slightest idea how to invent something. I'm so inadequate to do anything like that."

Sarah described what happened next as being like a lightning bolt. Instantly, in that moment, she knew exactly how to solve the problem. In fact, she saw an image in her head of a device and knew God wanted her to do something with what he was showing her.

"People think I'm crazy when I say this," she says today, "but it was like God was speaking into my ear. I knew what he was saying."

What Sarah heard God saying to her was this: "Sarah, Levi isn't the only one struggling like this. It's like when the Israelites were crying for help, and I sent Moses to deliver the message that set them free. I need you to be my Moses, because there are a lot of people struggling just like Levi, and I'm going to use you. I'm going to ask you to do a lot of things that are far beyond your natural abilities, so it can't be explained away. And I need you to say yes. I need you to be all in. If Medtronic or 3M or any other medical device company came up with this idea, it would make sense, but I'm not going to use them. I'm going to use you, Sarah Olson from Hugo, Minnesota, single mom of three. It won't make sense, but just do what I tell you to do. Have faith in me to guide you."

Sarah sketched the image onto paper. She watched YouTube videos to try to figure out how to make a CAD design to be printed by a 3D printer. Finally, she enlisted a friend who helped her complete the drawing and locate a 3D printer. When she had a prototype in hand, she made an appointment to see Dr. Vandersteen. Sitting in his office once again, she asked, "Remember when you told me I had to invent something?"

"Yes. But I was joking."

"But I wasn't," she responded. "I promised you we're not going to use that Foley again. So I invented something." She slid the device across the desk toward him.

The doctor looked at the device and then at Sarah. "Really? You invented something?"

She nodded and told the urologist what he already knew: that the Foley catheter uses an internal stabilizer—a liquid-filled balloon at the end of it—to keep it from slipping out of the bladder. That means there's something foreign inside the bladder.

"And the bladder doesn't like that," Sarah explained. "It leads to infections and bladder spasms. Miserable for anyone, especially kids."

Dr. Vandersteen looked interested. "Go on."

"That means we have to stabilize the darn thing from the outside," she said.

He had been studying the prototype. Sure enough, the external adhesive patch and long port—Levi called it a "lizard tongue"—would secure and stabilize a catheter outside of the body instead of inside the bladder.

The doctor's face lit up. "This will work."

"So can we use my invention on Levi instead of the Foley catheter?" she asked.

His answer to that was no. The catheter would have to have a patent first.

Sarah hadn't expected that. "A patent? How do I get a patent?"

"I don't know," he said. "But you figured this out. So go get it done."

The surgery to reopen Levi's stoma would take place in thirty-two days. Sarah began talking with anyone who would listen: "What do you know and who do you know that could help me get a patent for a medical device?" Eventually she met a patent developer, and they worked night and day writing an application for a patent. The device was approved for a provisional patent two days before Levi's surgery.

Dr. Vandersteen used the new device on Levi, and the results were nothing short of miraculous. After Levi's first stoma surgery, complications from the Foley catheter had resulted in his spending two and a half weeks in the hospital, six surgeries, a significant amount of drugs—and the stoma still hadn't healed up after six months.

This time, wearing the device his mother had invented for him, Levi spent one night in the hospital for observation, went home, and healed in ten days with no infections, complications, or bladder infections.

Back in Dr. Vandersteen's office a few weeks later, Sarah said, "We did it! That was amazing. And now we're done."

"As far as Levi goes, you're done," the doctor agreed. "But you're certainly not done. You now own the patent on a device that can help people and save lives all over the globe. You have a huge responsibility now. You need to take this device to market somehow."

Again Sarah felt perplexed. "What in the world does that mean?"

"I don't know. But if the big medical device companies catch wind of what you're doing, they won't be pleased because they don't want anything competing with the Foley. The Foley is a seven-billion-dollar industry—just that one catheter—because it's the only device that has been used. Until now. So you've got to do this by yourself. And nobody in the world has done that before."

Sarah continued praying—and asking everyone she met if they knew someone who could help her get the device into the marketplace. She began referring to her invention as the LECS, for Levi's External Catheter Stabilizer. She learned that an acquaintance knew the CEO of a medical device corporation. Treading carefully, she asked to meet with him to see if he had any advice. Sitting in front of the CEO's expansive, burnished desk, Sarah told her story, ending with a passionate plea: "What do I do next? How do I take a medical device to market?"

The CEO started laughing.

Feeling put off, she asked, "What are you laughing at?"

"Sarah," the CEO said, catching his breath, "you know what you remind me of?"

"What?"

"You remind me of a ferret on meth," he said.

Sarah blinked. "Excuse me?"

"You're so excited about something that's never going to happen," he continued. "You're in over your head. Just stop. Now. This isn't something that individuals do on their own. You're going to waste time. You're going to waste money. You're going to make a lot of people upset. You're going to ruin your reputation. The medical device field is brutal. They'll chew you up and spit you out."

As he was talking, Sarah was praying. Would this be the moment she would run into defeat? Or would she trust God to use her and her invention to bless others?

Calmly standing up, Sarah put her hands on the edge of the giant desk and leaned in. "You know what?" she said defiantly. "You might be the owner of a medical device company. You might know a lot more than I do. But you put your pants on the same way I do every morning, and if you can do it, so can I. And what you are saying to discourage me is only lighting a fire in me. I'm going to get this done. This medical device will be in hospitals someday, I promise you that. So I'm not mad at you. In fact, I thank you. Thank you for lighting a fire that is going to burn in my gut for the rest of my life." Picking up her purse and file folders, she turned and walked out of the office.

It wouldn't be the first meeting that she would turn on its ear.

Six months later, Sarah had attracted enough investors to put together a small team of consultants, accountants, and lawyers. Sitting around a boardroom table, they debated which of four types of elastomer—a rubbery, flexible material—the LECS should be made from.

It was a make-or-break decision. The wrong choice could cost tens of thousands of dollars that Sarah didn't have. She had a few investors, but there was always only enough money to be able to take the next step, never more than she needed; never enough to absorb an expensive mistake.

As the men and women around the table explained why one manufacturing material was the best, Sarah was struck by the irony of the situation. She thought, *I'm sitting at the head of this table, a mom with pink hair, surrounded by very smart people who know what they're doing, and I have no idea what they're talking about. And I'm going to have to make the final decision.*

After their members of the team finished their discussion about how to produce the product, Sarah said, "I'm going to step outside for five minutes, and when I come back, I'll tell you what we're going to do."

When Sarah returned, she said, "All right, everyone, we're going to go with option C. I can't tell you why, except that I prayed about it, and I know we're supposed to go with C."

A few people murmured.

"My faith is important to me," Sarah explained, "and I pray about every decision. And then I do what God tells me to do. And you're probably thinking, 'Why did she even hire us if she's not going to follow our advice?' Or maybe you're thinking, 'She's raised thousands of dollars of other people's money, and this is how she runs her business?' I get it. But God asked me right from the start to listen to Him and do what He tells me to do. And if that sounds crazy to you, you're free to go. No hard feelings."

Two people walked out. The rest stayed.

A couple of weeks later, the team reassembled, and one of the members said, "Well, we had no idea, but the company that made the elastomer we recommended wouldn't have [provided] the medical grade we would need. The material wouldn't have worked long term. Looks like option C was the right choice."

Sarah smiled. "I know it was."

The LECS brought relief and healing to Sarah's son. She says he still needs to use it occasionally and that it has helped him avoid surgery more than once.

Sarah believes that God worked overtime to make sure that Levi got what he needed—and is still working miracles within her company to make sure other children and adults get help, too. Within five years, Sarah's company, Levity Products, obtained a certificate of biocompatibility on the first attempt, meaning that the material used does not cause complications when applied to the body. The device passed clinical trials with no problems or delays, and she received patents on two additional medical devices.

"Big corporations spend ten years and ten million dollars to get where we are today," Sarah said. "God got us here in half the time with half the capital."

Recently, Levi was diagnosed with a rare spinal disease unrelated to spina bifida. Sarah says that despite living with debilitating pain, her ten-year-old is one of the most faith-filled, resilient people she's ever met.

One day she asked him, "How do you do it, buddy? How do you deal with this kind of pain and keep smiling?"

"Well, Mama," he answered, "life goes the way the corners of your mouth turn."

She asked what he meant.

He nodded. "If you smile, life goes better. So if I have the choice, why wouldn't I smile? And if I have the choice to complain or not to complain, I'm going to choose not to complain, because if my mind is complaining, my body is going to complain, too."

When days are hard for Levi or for Sarah, she remembers his sage advice and adds a twist of her own: "If I have the choice to pray and trust God—or the choice not to pray or trust Him—I'm going to pray and trust. Faith is a choice. And my journey has proved that faith in God is always the right choice."

A FUTURE FOR HAITI

With a Divine Assignment on her heart, a young woman
defies impossibility.

> "For I know the plans I have for you," declares the
> LORD, "plans to prosper you and not to harm you,
> plans to give you hope and a future."
>
> —JEREMIAH 29:11

*H*aiti, in the heart of the Caribbean, is a lush, sunny country. But it's also one of the most corrupt in the Western Hemisphere. An air of hopelessness hangs over any conversation about political reform. It seems as though no matter how much money is poured into Haiti, there will always be rampant disease, unfixed roads, unresolved problems. And if you walk down the street and talk with people, you'll never find anyone who will say, "I can't wait for the future." What future?

Knowing all of that, then, why would a young American woman feel she could make a difference? Britney Gengel was convinced that she could. No one believed that. That's because at nineteen, Britney was a teenager who hadn't quite found her purpose. The year before she went to Haiti, Britney had committed to taking a French experiential class but had backed out. Instead she spent the term on her college campus in Florida, working on her tan.

But as you'll see, God had quite the plan for her.

Britney landed in Haiti with a newfound focus for her life. She felt God's hand awakening compassion and optimism in her spirit. She was moved by the profound poverty she witnessed but also by the abundant faith and resilience possessed by the people of Haiti, especially the children.

She texted her parents on January 12, 2010, "They love us so much and everyone is so happy. They love what they have, and they work so hard to get nowhere, yet they are all so appreciative. I want to move here and start an orphanage myself."

That sounded great, but it would turn out to be one of her final text messages home. On that very same day, Haiti saw hell. It came in the form of a magnitude 7 earthquake, a disaster so sweeping and unexpected that it threw the island into chaos.

A major reason why the aftermath was so bad was that Haiti's infrastructure was already weak. Losing access to already limited running water and electricity was devastating, never mind the catastrophe of collapsing buildings. After the first tremor shook the capital, Port-au-Prince, one woman remembered her daughter asking "Are we going to die?" She simply said, "I don't have the answer to that, but if we're going to die, we'll die together." A Haitian psychologist remembered the horror of watching workers separate the dead into groups of children and adults. More than a decade later, parts of the collapsed nation have not been rebuilt, with aid funds funneled to unreliable companies by corrupt officials.[24]

As parents, what we often want more than anything else is to protect our kids from the harsher side of life, to preserve them as long as possible and keep them safe. But Britney's story—and the extraordinary things that happened next—reminds us that sometimes, when our kids encounter a dangerous world, God can use them in ways we couldn't have imagined. The story of how Britney's dream triumphed over tragedy and corruption serves as a shining example for all of us.

She wasn't perfect, but her loved ones say that's a reminder that the Lord chooses us in spite of our flaws. Britney's friends at Lynn University in Boca Raton described her as a "caring princess." She was beautiful, buoyant, and drew a lot attention. And Britney could get things done. Cherylann said, "Brit was complicated. She could be demanding, but she would also be the first person to lend you a hand. She was a genuine person with a heart of gold."

Britney would invite Cherylann to join her on outings with her friends, cajoling her mother when she declined the offer. Cherylann was pleased to be asked. "Brit was never ashamed of her father, Len, and me; she never hesitated to introduce us to her friends."

Len also remembers other sides of Britney, admiring his daughter's toughness. Once, Brit attended a high school basketball game in Worcester, Massachusetts, in an area of that city that had fallen on hard times. It was a classic "rich suburban kids" versus "poor urban kids" rivalry. After the game, Brit and her cheerleader friend Tara, on the advice of teachers, tried to get out of the parking lot and home as soon as possible. Brit's school had been victorious, and the losing side was spoiling for a fight. Spotting Tara's uniform, a group surrounded Brit's car, pounded it with their fists, and taunted her and the other occupants. As Brit said, "I got out of the car and started swinging."

Len and Cherylann didn't sleep well that night. They never advocated for violence as a solution, and they were grateful that the outcome (Brit's bruised and swollen cheek) hadn't been worse.

As Len put it, "We always told her that nobody can take your dignity from you. Those kids had crossed a line with her."

Brit crossed another line while at Lynn University her sophomore year. She approached Len and Cherylann to let them know that for January Term, or J-Term (a four-week period at the beginning of the spring semester when students can take classes or do volunteer work to earn credits), she had decided that she wanted to join a group of classmates and professors in Haiti. At first her parents were dubious, given the fact that she had given up the previous year on her commitment to that French class.

This year, she was determined to commit to something for real.

One of Britney's friends, Lindsay, had gone to Haiti the year prior and was returning. She said the experience had been life changing.

"I want to go," Britney told her parents. "I have to go."

Len and Cherylann did their due diligence. Along with Lynn University, the program was a part of Food for the Poor. The students would be safe and well supervised. They were pleased by the assurances they received and by Brit's strongly expressed desire to go somewhere to be of help to others. The Gengels were practicing Catholics, and although they'd moved away from Len's hometown of Worcester, they still attended Mass at St. John's every Sunday. One of the lessons they learned was to be of service to others.

Among their ways of giving back was that every year at

Christmas the entire Gengel family would participate in a Christmas charity program. Len and Cherylann were a real success story—he with his construction company and she with a restaurant. They believed in the importance of giving back to the community, remaining grounded and grateful, making a difference in the lives of others.

Britney followed those examples of making a difference in the lives of people who needed help. She went to Haiti with the Journey of Hope team. The experience was transformative. So were the photographs Len and Cherylann later saw of her. They were all images of a radiant Brit as she sat among a group of young orphans, their arms entwined.

On January 12, 2010, Cherylann got a check-in call from Brit. She described her day: a morning at an orphanage and an afternoon at an eldercare center. The former had been wonderful, the latter less so. A woman at the eldercare home had challenged Brit and the others' intentions. She believed that it was easy for them to come to Haiti for a few days, do a few good works, and then leave, absent of guilt but also absent of commitment. A few days later, the woman accused them—they'd be back home in the United States and would likely forget about what they'd seen.

Cherylann heard the fierce determination in her daughter's voice when she said, "I just sat there and took it and kept helping the other people. We won them over. They knew we weren't there pitying them. We just wanted to help them. No judging."

Three hours before the fateful earthquake Brit had sent a text message that ended, "I want to move here and start an orphanage myself."

Those were the last words Britney Gengel would ever share with Len and Cherylann. She, along with five other members of the Lynn University contingent, perished in the earthquake. Len and Cherylann endured the worst days of their lives. At first, they received assurances that Brit was among the survivors. When that report proved wrong, they waited an agonizing thirty-three days before their daughter's body was recovered and returned to them. Len had traveled to Haiti to see for himself if the rescue, and then recovery, operations were overwhelmed.

As a news anchor, I was on the air covering the breaking details of the horror in Haiti. Images poured in from wire services and disaster relief organizations. Haiti looked like a meteorite had hit from outer space. The United Nations announced that 102 of its staff members lost their lives, among the reported 220,000 people killed.

I can only imagine the hopelessness that Britney's parents must have felt when they witnessed the chaos and destruction for themselves. One night, Len recalls viewing from a distance the rubble that had once been the hotel his daughter and the other members of the Lynn University group had stayed in. Len looked at the sky and had a long conversation with his daughter. He acknowledged that the two of them argued over the years and, he told Brit that he appreciated the last text that she'd sent her mom. He took some comfort in knowing that she had been maturing into the kind of young woman he'd hoped she'd become and that as parents they'd done the right things most of the time.

Most of all, Len wanted her to know this: "I will be back to honor your last wish someday. I promise you!"

Obviously, it is one thing to say that you would like to build an orphanage to help children and another thing entirely to do it. To say that Len, Cherylann, and their boys took on a monumental task is an understatement. That they were able to do it, with the help of hundreds of volunteers and supporters in a country like Haiti, is miraculous.

According to the logic of the world, Len and Cherylann were being foolish. They should have left such things to experts. But as Paul reminds us, "God chose the foolish things of the world to shame the wise; God chose the weak things of the world to shame the strong. God chose the lowly things of this world and the despised things—and the things that are not—to nullify the things that are, so that no one may boast before him." (1 Corinthians 1:27–29)

Len was no professional mission worker. But he did know how to do one thing: construction. He had spent his entire adult life in construction; he was driven; he immersed himself in action; and he would not be deterred when it came to making certain that his daughter's wish would be fulfilled.

"God's blueprints are so massive and so all-encompassing that we can't possibly see every detail and every perspective and every elevation and every floor plan at one time. He can." Len's words reveal both his faith in God and his many years in construction. Both of those helped the Gengel family realize Brit's dream.

He began plans to build an orphanage.

Len and Cherylann are people of faith, and they both have a simple expression for what they believe: "God is love." The people of Haiti continue to need both God's love and ours. Following the devastating earthquake in 2010, that same year a deadly cholera outbreak ravaged the country. In 2016, Hurricane Matthew dealt a horrific blow to the nation, leaving more than a million Haitians in need of assistance. Now, six years after that, poverty, political unrest, and violence continue to be major problems in a beautiful country that has a long history of being victimized by natural disasters and human greed.

The idea for the orphanage came to Len when he shared photographs of Brit's experience with their parish priest. "Father Madden saw the pictures we shared with him of Brit the day before the earthquake. She was so happy and smiling and surrounded by so many young kids. They all looked so happy that day, but what happened to them after the earthquake? Father Madden said, 'Who's going to take care of these children?' That question was the kickoff of things for me."

In retrospect, Cherylann sees God's hand at work in all of this. "Who else but Len could have led us on this mission and done what we did as quickly as we did? I mean, he didn't have any experience in creating a not-for-profit foundation, but with all our connections and ties to the community and our commitment to Brit's dream, we made that happen. The rest? The site selection, the design and engineering plans, the blueprints, overseeing the work itself, that was what Len did for years and years.

"My faith tells me that we're all put here on this earth to do good works. Whether we choose to do them or not is up to us. How we chose to deal with our daughter's death wasn't predetermined. We had choices to make, and we chose what we chose not just because of what Brit texted but because what she wanted aligned with what we've believed all along: God is love. And if you love God, you love his people; you do whatever you can to help them. You be of service. You use the skills and the tools that you have developed to not just help your own family but the family of God."

The story of the Lynn University students' deaths in the Haiti earthquake made national headlines. Donations to the Gengel family started to arrive from people they didn't know. Cherylann was grateful for the outpouring of support for them but saw it as part of a bigger plan. Even without those donations they were determined to build their not-for-profit foundation, the Be Like Brit Foundation, but they certainly helped.

Within the span of eight months the Gengels purchased land in Grand Goâve, Haiti, to begin construction on the orphanage less than a year after the earthquake, and with the aid of donations and volunteers, they completed the construction of a state-of-art, earthquake-secure facility in two years, welcoming the first child to the orphanage shortly thereafter.

By the end of 2014, they welcomed their sixty-sixth child. From the outset, they had envisioned a facility that could care for sixty-six children, one boy and one girl for each of the thirty-three days from the time of the earthquake to Brit's body being recovered.

As Len says, "One of my catchphrases throughout our journey with Brit's passing and with our efforts to see her dream realized in full has been 'You can't make this stuff up.' And I wouldn't report these things if they weren't true. It wasn't me who made the connection that Brit's ordeal, our ordeal in seeing her body be recovered and returned, took thirty-three days and that Jesus walked the earth for that many years. I'm not comparing my daughter to our Savior, and maybe those numbers are just a coincidence in some people's minds, but they mean something to me."

There were more meaningful coincidences as the Gengels' plans moved forward. In the early stages of the development of what would become Brit's Home, the Haitian government put up roadblock after roadblock. Frustrated and wondering where to turn, Len and Cherylann were shocked when their son Bernie told them that he'd had a fortuitous roommate assignment change for his second year at college. The young man moving in was the son of the president of Haiti. Roadblocks became routes. Hindrances became helping hands.

The couple experienced a number of reminders that God was there to help. Shortly before the family moved out of the house that Brit had been raised in—the family needed to scale back in order to help fund their plan—Len was making a last pass in a closet in the bedroom he and Cherylann shared. He was on his hands and knees looking on the floor when he stood up and hit his head on a collection of hangers. He pushed them aside and noticed something draped and wound over the bar. It glittered in the light. When he unfurled it, he held a pair of angel's wings made of gold-plated metal and wire. He'd never seen them before, and when he asked Cherylann about them she told him that she hadn't, either. "Well, I guess Brit left you a present."

For Len it was as though God had left him a reminder of His and Brit's presence in his life. "When you lose a child . . . it takes the life out of you," he said. "You don't really heal. You learn how to function."

For the next two years after discovering those wings, Len carried them with him when he made more than thirty trips to Haiti to oversee various aspects of the planning and construction of the orphanage. He and his wife have countless stories of other "angels" who intervened in all aspects of their endeavor, from contractors in the United States who donated their time to work on the plumbing or electrical work to the owner of a car dealership who recognized Len at a Boston airport, shared the story of the loss of his own son, and later mailed a $10,000 donation when he wasn't able to secure a box truck to carry tools and supplies to the site in Haiti.

Len has been inspired by the Haitians he's hired who did the bulk of the work on the facility and now run the operation. Initially, he was wary that corruption might impede the work. But his experience has been quite the wonderful opposite. He's found the people of Haiti he's contacted and worked with to be enormously cooperative, completely above board, and inspiring.

Once, when a wire transfer of funds didn't arrive in time to pay the construction workers, a trusted manager transferred money out of his own account to make certain that the workers would be paid on time. Later, in what Len chalked up to be a miracle, they finally managed to secure a deal with a materials service provider to bring concrete on site and pump it onto the roof. To that point, they'd done all the concrete work the old-fashioned way, mixing it by hand or using a small mixer. The concrete roof, so essential to creating a stable, earthquake-resistant building, required an enormous amount of concrete. Even having secured the use of the pumper trucks, it would still take sixty straight hours of labor to complete the roof. Len considers that effort to be the most amazing he's ever experienced.

He got very little sleep throughout that period. Later, he discovered that the last remnants of the angel's wings had fallen from his pocket and into the wet concrete of the roof. The wings had served their purpose and gotten them all to that crucial point in the construction. He was sad to lose them but grateful for what they'd helped to achieve. He said, "Those golden wings were now a permanent part of the building, and instead of feeling the loss of the angel's wings, I felt more strongly Brit's presence. I'd lost something but gained so much more in return."

Like Britney, Len believed he was going to Haiti to give something to the people there. Instead, like her, he understands now he's actually been the recipient of a precious gift. He's been captivated by the spirit of the people of Haiti and the abiding faith they have in God. As Brit noted in her text home, he's seen their generosity and their gratitude.

He said, "I went to Haiti thinking 'I'm going to build this building. I'm going to honor my daughter's last wish and turn that heartache into hope.' I found out that . . . there was a greater purpose than just doing what my daughter wanted. We were helping to heal our own loss, our own suffering, but we were doing far more than that."

His faith tells him that Britney is enjoying eternal life, and he hopes to join her in that life someday. More immediately, though, he says, "My faith got me through something so horrible, so brutal, that if I didn't have faith, I would never have gotten through."

Another thing that bolsters Len's faith is that he is no stranger to miracles in his own life. He has had several near-death experiences.

One of those experiences would later come to mean something far different. It happened in 2006, when Len, who had had heart trouble for many years, passed out on the floor. He was going toward the light. Suddenly his late mother and father appeared, took him by each elbow, and began guiding him forward.

"I was resisting. I kept saying I wasn't ready. 'The kids are too young.' It was beautiful to be there, but I wasn't ready," he remembers. "I had to be there for the kids. At the time I was thinking of my three kids, but as it turned out, there were a lot more kids to care for, an entire community and beyond."

Caring for those kids has meant that Len's life has been transformed. He no longer runs his construction company. Instead, he devotes all his time to the Be Like Brit Foundation and is known as "Papi Len" to the children living at Brit's Home in Grand Goâve. Cherylann is also full-time at the foundation as executive director. Their elder son, Bernie, also works for the foundation, serving in many capacities including, informally, as the chief technology officer, not just helping to teach computer literacy and programming skills to the children but utilizing social media and other facets of twenty-first-century technology to enrich their educational experiences and offer them hope for a better employment future.

It would have been easy for them to rest on their laurels, but they have overseen the evolution of the programs and the facilities at Brit's Home for the past twelve years. They quickly realized that Haitians in the community surrounding their orphanage desperately needed help, too—help they could provide. Their fundamental mission hasn't changed so much as it has expanded. They provide clean water for many in the community, so they don't have to walk long distances to reach it.

In addition to providing for the sixty-six children, Len and Cherylann now employ more than a hundred individuals in the community. As Len points out, the United Nations has conducted studies that show that in Haiti, if one person is earning a sustainable salary, he or she spreads the wealth and ten families are able to eat healthfully as a result. Because of the generosity of private donations and sponsors, they've also constructed 154 homes for formerly impoverished members of the community.

Just as important, the Gengels started a program that has seen more than 2,400 individuals, many of them students like Brit was, who have come to Haiti to help with the construction of those structures and otherwise assist in the operation. In many cases, the experience of those "Britsionarys" has transformed their lives. Len and Cherylann have received dozens of emails from former participants who have described the powerful impact the experience has had on them. Some have decided to change majors to pursue careers in education, counseling, and other forms of public service. Some have been so inspired by the work they've seen being done in Haiti that they've chosen to major in international development to take what they've seen working in Grand Goâve to other locations around the world.

Len's perspective has also evolved, "When you lose a child, you cling to many things, often to bitterness and despair. . . . Since the earthquake, I've run into a number of people, many of [whom] professed their faith in God, who have said to me that it must be comforting to know that God had a plan for Brit. In a sense, what some of them have said to me is that God took Brit from us. I don't believe that, not one bit. God didn't kill my daughter and those thousands of other people. That's unfathomable. What happened was a natural disaster, and we all make choices and they have consequences.

"Just as I can't tell anyone how they should grieve the loss of their child, I can't tell anyone what to believe. All I know is that we've chosen to get up every day and put one foot in front of the other, and we chose to build this memorial to honor our daughter, to fulfill her last wish, to help children in Haiti. That's why I carried those wings with me for so long, to serve as a reminder of what my focus should be. When Brit first sent that text, she, and we, had no way of knowing that she was sending a light that would help us through the darkness."

That light is why those sixty-six children have hope for a brighter future. Children such as Ephesiens, Christ-Love, Kathiana, Magdeline, and others have a vision of possibility because a young woman saw possibility and not just poverty. The light she shined through the darkness has been reflected time and time again.

Jesus said, "Whatever you did for one of the least of these brothers and sisters of mine, you did for me." (Matthew 25:40) It's so easy to turn away our eyes from the needs of the world, thinking they're someone else's problem, someone else's area of expertise. But Jesus calls us to use what skills we have and to learn the ones we don't.

When we care for the least of these, we often find that, in doing so, we get back so much more than we gave. It can heal the broken places in us.

ADDICTION WON'T WIN

God uses a woman's weakness, her seventeen-year heroin
addiction, to reveal her purpose!

> If I say, "Surely the darkness will hide me and the
> light become night around me,"
> even the darkness will not be dark to you; the
> night will shine like the day, for darkness is as light
> to you.
>
> —PSALM 139:11–12

"What are you going to do with the baby?" the young woman asked casually across the bar as she stirred her drink.

DeEtte, seven months pregnant, sold drugs from behind the counter. She shrugged. "You know. Probably give it up for adoption."

DeEtte had given birth to two other children, one of whom had been born addicted to heroin. DeEtte guessed that this baby would be born addicted, too. She hadn't kept the first two; she knew she couldn't keep this one, either.

"Well, my brother and his wife have been trying to adopt for years," the young woman said over the loud music. "I bet they would love to take the baby,"

"Yeah, they could have her."

"Great! Let me give them a call right now."

Later that night, DeEtte met up with John and Lupe at a Denny's restaurant, where she agreed to hand over the baby.

All she asked in exchange was to be put up in a motel until the baby was born. It would be good to have a bed and a hot shower for a change.

DEETTE HAS LIVED IN DARK places few of us will ever visit. But her life didn't start out that way. DeEtte was born in 1954 on Marine Corps Logistics Base Barstow in southern California's Mojave Desert. Her father loved his five children, but he also loved other women than his wife. When DeEtte was ten, her mom left her dad, taking the kids and moving back to her native island of Oahu, Hawaii.

Relatives took them in while DeEtte's mother landed a job and worked the night shift to save up for their own place. But at night, when her mother was away, DeEtte's uncle made his way into DeEtte's room. She was molested by her uncle for months before the family moved to the Harbor City projects in Los Angeles.

Reeling from the abuse, DeEtte desperately wanted to fit in and find acceptance—but the Harbor City projects offered very few good options. Poverty, drugs, and crime formed a destructive alliance that ruled the neighborhoods. Given DeEtte's Hawaiian heritage, everyone mistook her for a Latina, so she eventually just embraced it. Joining a Mexican gang gave her a sense of family, and before long she was ditching school and trading textbooks for booze and weed.

By age fourteen, a petty theft conviction landed her in the local juvenile detention center. By age sixteen, she got pregnant by a rival gang member, who died of an overdose around the time she gave birth to their son, Trinidad. For four years, DeEtte's mother raised the baby, who was eventually adopted by his father's parents. Desperate to bury the pain of that first childish romance, DeEtte turned to harder drugs. Jealous of other girls at school who had the money for clothes, she started stealing so she'd have something to wear.

Life was hard, and heroin became her anesthetic. She had a second baby, this time with a drug dealer running dope from Mexico to the United States. At the time, she was shooting about $1,000 a day of uncut heroin. After her boyfriend went to prison, their daughter, born addicted to heroin, was adopted by the father's sister, Elsa.

For a while, DeEtte sold herself as what she called a "high-class prostitute," traveling to places where she could make big money. She went to Las Vegas and charged clients $1,000 an hour. But that didn't last long. She ended up working at a bar, where she met the woman who arranged her third child's adoption.

But before long, DeEtte was pregnant and incarcerated—again. John and Lupe visited DeEtte in jail and pleaded for her to let them adopt this fourth baby, too. They promised to name her Danielle, after DeEtte's sister. They had already named DeEtte's other child after her birth mother.

"At first I told them no," DeEtte remembered. "I wanted to believe that when I got out this time, I was going to go straight, and maybe keeping this baby would help me clean up my life. But in the end, I gave them that baby, too, because deep in my heart I knew I wasn't going to clean up. I knew I couldn't give this—or any—child a decent life."

EACH TIME SHE WENT TO jail, DeEtte had plenty of time to think longingly of her children and to regret her choices in life—especially since she was in the habit of starting riots and often found herself in an isolation cell. In 1971, she had an experience that meant she could never again pretend that God wasn't real. One day when she was working the streets, she heard music from a local Christian group, Addicts for Christ, which drew her to approach them. "Right then and there, I got hit with the Holy Spirit," she said. She felt her heart overflowing with joy, but the next morning, she woke up sick from heroin. While she kept going back to that charity for worship, "it's like I had one foot in, one foot out." Despite God's urging to tell other people about Him, she felt embarrassed.

"I had a reputation," she said. "You know, people look up to you and respect you because you know how to do time. You're hard core, you don't snitch, you don't show weakness. . . . I did not want people to know I was weak and I had turned Christian."

Instead, she had gone deep into sin, doing things she'd never dreamed she would do. She believed in the spiritual world—particularly in demons—but it took until 1986 for her to have a "real experience with Jesus."

One day, in the process of being incarcerated yet again, she found herself sitting on a wooden bench in the holding tank, waiting for paperwork to be completed so she could be locked up for another two years. She was already sweating and aching and shivering from withdrawal.

As more women were brought into the holding tank for processing, DeEtte was struck by how many seemed to be in their seventies and beyond. Those old addicts were regulars. They'd been there many times.

As had she.

And that shook her. *I don't want to still be doing this when I'm seventy*, she thought.

DeEtte's grandmother and aunt believed in God, and DeEtte had childhood memories of hearing them singing and praying. They believed that God answered prayers. DeEtte wanted desperately to believe that, too.

A month before she was scheduled to be released, she started praying: "God, I know you're real. And I don't want to come back to prison. I'm so tired of it all. I'm tired of the drugs. Tired of the lifestyle. Tired of the bravado and desperation and pain. If you can change me, God, please do!"

The day she walked out of prison, she had a feeling that she wouldn't be back and felt a strange sorrow. Starting from the time she was just a kid, DeEtte had been sentenced to jail or prison more than a dozen times. Orange County Central Jail had been a kind of home for more than a decade. Many of her fellow inmates had had childhoods like hers, and everyone was trying to mask their pain, trying to pretend it was all okay when it clearly was not. So they swapped stories, joked together, and passed around family photos of happier times. They were a forgotten, eclectic group of convicts—yet they were family.

Within hours of her release, DeEtte was high again, embracing her old lifestyle of addiction and prostitution with open arms. But she had truly hit rock bottom. Gone were the high-end days, now she was back on the streets of Orange County doing five-dollar tricks just to pay for a fix.

IT CAN BE EASY TO look at other people and not really see them. Someone on the subway dressed in a way we would never dress—he or she can't be the same as you and me, a person created in God's image. People in sitcoms and movies never think about God, never talk about the spiritual realities underlying the world around them. It's easy to think that people in real life are that shallow, too. But in reality, most of us contemplate those questions.

There are moments when we feel as though we've made so many mistakes that there's nothing God can do to reach us, that we can't reach for something higher.

That was how DeEtte felt. God would need to show her it was possible; He would need to show her that she mattered to Him.

Six months after her release, DeEtte was unlocking the front door to her duplex when she heard sirens. She had just finished shooting up when someone began pounding on her door.

"DeEtte!" a neighbor screamed. "Someone ran over Marla! Someone ran over Marla!"

DeEtte's niece, Marla, attended elementary school a few blocks from DeEtte's apartment. DeEtte ran the entire distance just in time to see the little seven-year-old loaded into the ambulance. Walking across the street after school, the second grader had gotten distracted chasing a page of homework being blown by the wind and had stepped in front of a car.

"I knew my sister Danielle was on her way to the hospital," DeEtte recalled. "I was still in a heavy drug stupor—so I went home to finish shooting up before going downtown to the hospital."

When DeEtte walked into the waiting room an hour later, it was packed with more than thirty people from Danielle's church, Victory Outreach in Santa Ana, California. They were crying and holding each other and reaching their hands toward Danielle in prayer.

Marla had just been pronounced dead.

"The emotions in that room overwhelmed me," DeEtte said.

"I began to weep—for Marla, but also for me. I felt such sorrow and loss in that space—but at the same time, such love and peace. And I felt something else, too, something I'd been longing for, something I'd been searching for all my life."

Three nights later, DeEtte attended a viewing for Marla at the funeral home. Again the room overflowed with members of Danielle's church. And again the power of love and the presence of God in the place nearly brought DeEtte to her knees.

Suddenly she did a double take. "I began to see people I knew, people I'd done drugs with or served time with," she said. "They were people I'd run with on the street I hadn't seen in so long I'd thought they had died."

A woman approached who had once shared a cell block with her. "DeEtte?"

"Evelyn?" DeEtte gasped. "Why are you here?"

"I know Danielle from church."

The two women hugged and cried, sharing their disbelief over Marla's death. Before Evelyn left, she said, "DeEtte, I want you to know that Jesus loves you. He saved me. He freed me. My life is completely different now. He can do the same for you."

A man approached DeEtte. They had bought and sold drugs together years before. His face glowed. In fact, he seemed transformed in every way.

"DeEtte," he said, clasping her hands. "God is real. God is good, you know?"

DeEtte saw another familiar face, this time belonging to a woman she had once worked the streets with. The woman ran up and embraced DeEtte in a bear hug. "DeEtte," she said through tears, "Jesus changed my life. And what he did for me, I know he can do for you, too."

"I saw the love of Jesus in those people," DeEtte recalled. "I saw how they had loved my niece, how they loved my sister. And it was that love that brought me to God. I was sick and tired of the lifestyle. They were clean, they were happy, and I wanted what they had."

The next day, DeEtte checked herself into Victory Outreach, a faith-based rehab program in La Puente, California, where she stayed for the next three years. After suffering through withdrawal for a couple weeks, she dived deeper into prayer, often sneaking away to a shed on the property where, in solitude, she cried out to Heaven:

Why did my life turn out this way?
How did I become such a horrible person?
Why did my dad leave?
Why did my uncle abuse me?
Why did all those other men strip me of all decency?

"I had so much guilt inside of me and, and I feel so ugly about myself," she said. But God "showed me . . . it was like a strip of a movie show, flashing in front of me from when I was a little girl, baby, till that moment in the shed."

Flashbacks of experiences that DeEtte had forgotten flooded her mind. She saw all the faces of the men who had treated her inhumanely. Then she heard a quiet but powerful voice in her soul: Forgive them. Just forgive them.

It wasn't instantaneous, and it certainly wasn't easy. She spent hours in the shed, remembering and shedding all of the bad things done to her. Long prayers and cascades of tears accompanied the process—but she said it felt as though with each one, a great weight dropped off her soul. "I felt such freedom and liberty," she said.

There was a vision for the future, too. During those prayerful hours in the shed, DeEtte felt strongly that God was telling her that she would become a missionary, that He would restore to her that which had been lost, and that one day she would marry. All three seemed unlikely, if not impossible.

As DeEtte continued to heal in mind, body, and spirit, she had to learn skills she had never bothered to learn, such as how to use a checkbook, keep a job, pay her bills. At the encouragement of the rehab center staff, she became involved with service activities at Victory Outreach church. Soon she was helping out with the greeting team, choir, children's ministry, study groups, and homeless assistance.

The Lord had also given her a love for Hispanic people. She wondered for a while whether He meant her to work in Mexico, but in 1989, when DeEtte had the opportunity to help run a rehab home for addicts in Spain, she remembered the three promises God had made to her in the prayer shed, bought a ticket, and boarded a plane to Barcelona.

ONE DAY THE PASTOR OF the church running the rehab center in Barcelona pulled DeEtte aside. "That young woman can't come here anymore," he said gently.

DeEtte understood his position. Strung out on drugs, a young local woman had checked into the rehab center several times. But on Sundays, when the church was filled with worshippers, the woman caused havoc, stealing purses and even ripping gold necklaces from the necks of older parishioners.

DeEtte's heart broke with compassion for the twenty-two-year-old drug addict, who reminded her so much of herself. "Please, Pastor, let me work with her. I'll take full responsibility and blame for anything she does. I know God can help her. Please let me try!"

She convinced him, then found the woman in the parking lot and brought her back inside. They spent hours talking over bowls of paella, a thick stew of rice and seafood.

DeEtte recalled what the woman had said. "As tears streamed down her face, she kept saying to me in Spanish, 'I'm tired, I'm so tired of doing drugs and living this life. If God can change my life, if he can really change me, that's what I want.'"

DeEtte remembered similar prayers of her own the last time she had been in prison. "When she said she was tired of it all," she said, "I knew she was finally ready."

AFTER BEING A MISSIONARY FOR two years in Barcelona, DeEtte flew home to California. Within a few days, she got a phone call from Lupe. "DeEtte!" she cried excitedly. "I heard you were back in town! I found your other daughter! Her name is Lucy!"

"What? When? How?"

Lupe explained that six months earlier, she and John had taken the girls to the park for a Fourth of July picnic. She had been calling the children from the playground to come eat their lunch when a woman had approached. She'd had a child with her who appeared a little older than DeEtte, then six, and Danielle, five.

"I heard you call your daughter DeEtte," the woman commented, "It's a beautiful name. Where did you find it?'"

"I named her after her birth mother," Lupe explained. "Both of my girls are adopted."

The woman pursed her lips. "The birth mother. Was she on drugs? Was she Hawaiian?"

Lupe nodded in surprise.

"My name is Elsa," the woman said with a smile, "and I have her daughter, Lucy."

As Lupe finished telling DeEtte the story, she added that the two families had already become fast friends and the three little girls were growing up as true sisters.

"Lupe," DeEtte said gratefully, "John told me once that you and he prayed for years for a daughter and that God sent me to give you not one but two. When I was in prison, sometimes all I could think about was trying to get my children back so we could be a family. But God has given me such peace. And when things like this happen, I see His hand putting everything together."

BECAUSE OF THE SIGNIFICANT ABUSE DeEtte had suffered, marriage to a man seemed like an impossibility. "I didn't want anything to do with men. And when I met Jesus, I just wanted Jesus. And that's it." But after moving to San Antonio and attending Castle Hills Christian Church for a month, DeEtte was approached by a woman who said she wanted to introduce her to a man. DeEtte told her she wasn't interested, but that night, she couldn't get his name out of her head. She couldn't focus on anything, even prayer. She felt as though she was losing her mind. Finally, she called her pastor's wife and told her what was going on. The woman's reaction shocked her. She laughed.

"De, the day you walked into our church, I felt like God told me, 'She's going to marry Dan Faubel.'"

DeEtte was in shock.

"You should at least meet him!"

On their first coffee date, DeEtte and Dan talked for six hours. And as they did, DeEtte wondered if this was the fulfillment of the third promise God had made to her in her prayer shed. God had, indeed, taken her to the mission field and was helping her restore lost relationships with her children. Was he now inviting her into a healthy, loving marriage relationship with a husband he had prepared for her?

At first glance, the man sitting in front of her in cowboy boots and jeans wasn't at all like the style-conscious men she'd been drawn to in the past. But if she'd learned anything by now, it was that sometimes the best answers to prayers are the ones you never expected at all.

DEETTE IS SITTING IN THE living room with Dan, drinking coffee. They read a page from a devotional book and prayed over the coming day. The early-morning tradition has come to mean a lot to the couple throughout their twenty-five-year marriage.

These days, most of DeEtte's work helping addicts takes place in the United States. She stays in touch with the young woman from Spain, who is drug free and raising a family with her husband, a pastor, in Barcelona.

After Dan leaves for work, DeEtte lingers over her coffee. The cell phone beside her vibrates with an incoming text, and she smiles as she reads the bright "Good morning" message from one of her children.

Putting her coffee cup into the dishwasher, DeEtte thanks God for answered prayers and readies herself for a brand-new day.

THE POWER OF A PEANUT

A man learned to trust the Lord's vision and timing and it
changed what the world eats, even today.

The fear of the LORD is the beginning of wisdom,
and knowledge of the Holy One is understanding.
—PROVERBS 9:10

The answer was right out of sight. Professor George Washington
Carver had spent the afternoon sorting through odds and
ends. A colorful variety of plants was splayed across the top of his
desk, stems and petals and roots dissected neatly into their constit-
uent parts.

George loved to talk about nature to anyone who would listen, and by that point in his life had had a willing audience for
his knowledge: the students of the Tuskegee Institute. That day,
however, he was having a conversation with the most important
audience of all: his heavenly Father.

The subject of discussion was a botanical mystery. As George surveyed the plants before him, his eye had come to rest on a common nut deemed so useless that most farmers simply used it as fertilizer to replenish the soil after it was exhausted by cotton growing. But George's lifelong philosophy had been that God never created worthless things. He closed his eyes and prayed to the Lord, "Why did you make the peanut? Why?"[25] The answer to that question would revolutionize American agriculture and bring healing in the wake of a great conflict. And it all started with a humble prayer.

In a way, it was a prayer George had been offering up his whole life. Born into slavery, he had experienced a far different upbringing from most enslaved people of his era. First, he had never been to the South, having been born in Diamond Grove (now Diamond), Missouri. Second, he had never really lived as a slave.

Not long after George's birth, he, his sister, and his mother were kidnapped by marauders and taken to neighboring Kansas. At some point in the terrifying journey, baby George was separated from Mary. It's unclear whether the kidnappers intended to resell the child and mother or if they had other plans for them. But the kidnappers left George with a group of women in Kansas. When a stranger arrived and took the baby away, the women offered little resistance.

George later discovered that the stranger was a Union scout. But the baby's troubles weren't over; he still had to weather cold nights wrapped in the man's coat as they crossed back into Missouri. To make things worse, George had developed whooping cough, which could be deadly even for adults.

But there was good news. The scout, John Bentley, was taking George home. He was in the employ of George's master, Moses Carver, and when they arrived back in Diamond Grove, Moses gave Bentley an expensive racehorse in exchange for the safe return of the baby. George was home. But he would never see his mother again.

The trouble and expense to which Moses had gone to retrieve George was indicative of his character. Surprisingly, Moses and his wife didn't believe in slavery (they had made an exception to purchase George's mother as a servant), and when the Civil War had broken out, they had sided with the North.

So when Moses discovered where young George had ended up, getting him back became a rescue effort. Moses and his wife were childless, but when Moses's brother and his wife died, they took in their three children, two girls and a boy. They also raised George and his older half brother, James, as the fourth and fifth siblings of the family.

Young George was frequently sick, perhaps due to the whooping cough he'd had when he was rescued. The cough damaged his vocal cords, giving him a characteristic rasp that eventually strengthened into a more normal but still high-pitched voice.

So often it is the weak among us who are aware of God's mercy and faithfulness. And perhaps it was that infirmity that lent strength to George's mighty faith. George came to Jesus in spite of Moses Carver's influence. His foster father rejected religion, but George was highly devout, becoming aware of God at eight years old.

He was also fascinated by the natural world and was known to hoard interesting stones and fungi. And flowers. *What makes things grow?* The question had always occupied George's busy mind. He spent hours in the woods around Diamond Grove, stuffing his pockets with various rocks and gently easing wildflowers out of the dirt.

"Just plain foolishness." That was what the people of the

neighborhood said of the spindly boy who ran around with fists full of flowers, bending the ear of anyone who would listen with a wealth of facts about the natural world. *Foolishness. Waste of time. Why can't he turn his mind to important things?*

He later wrote, "Day after day I spent in the woods alone in order to collect my floral beauties and put them in my little garden I had hidden in the brush not far from the house, as it was considered foolishness in the neighborhood to waste time on flowers." [26] One day, of course, his intense focus on God's creation, deemed "foolishness" by his neighbors, would reap great benefits.

Always bright and curious, George loved learning and excelled when given the chance to attend school. Later, he was well on his way to a successful career as a professor at the Agricultural College of Iowa or some other notable institution when he was approached by Booker T. Washington, the founder of one of the first academic institutions for free Black people. Washington approached him about coming to the South, teaching at his newly formed Tuskegee Institute in Alabama, and exploring what they could do to help former slaves create better lives for themselves. George agreed, despite the smaller salary that came with it, and boarded a train for Tuskegee.

The trip provided his first glimpse of what life was like in the South three decades after the Civil War ended. The war had devastated the economy, and people were struggling to recover. Because of his expertise in agriculture, one of the first things he saw was that the single-crop economy of the South—cotton—was depleting not only the soil but also the people. Sharecroppers and tenant farmers grew cotton right up to the edges of their house to earn money and had room to grow little else.

Because of that, they had to buy food from general stores

owned by the same people who owned the land they worked. If they wanted to produce more, they had to buy expensive artificial fertilizers from those same stores. The longer and harder they worked, the more indebted they became. It was a vicious downward spiral.

George described that discovery:

> When my train left the golden wheat fields and the tall, green corn of Iowa for the acres of cotton, nothing but cotton, my heart sank a little. Not much evidence of scientific farming anywhere. The scraggy cotton grew close up to the cabin doors; a few lonesome collards, the only sign of vegetables; stunted cattle, boney mules; fields and hill sides cracked and scarred with gullies and deep ruts. Everything looked hungry: the land, the cotton, the cattle, and the people.[27]

Recognizing that hardship assured him that his decision to teach at Tuskegee had been the right one. He vowed to do everything within his power to help those farmers. One of the first things he did upon arrival was help set up an agricultural experiment station.

Though George was a skilled scientist by training, he took a different approach to his research from the typical scientific method. The scientific method requires sequentially documenting one variable at a time and seeing what effect changing each variable has. It starts with the formulation of a thesis and then sets about methodically proving or disproving it. Each study has to be carefully documented, so it can be replicated and tested again by others in various settings.

George understood that but also felt it was a slow, cumbersome process. Instead, he mixed the sequential method with intuition and inspiration—and with the faith that had sustained him through his life thus far. He would later tell audiences that God revealed the secrets He had hidden in nature to anyone willing to look long and hard enough. Thus, in the pursuit of breakthroughs, prayer became a more dependable companion for George than logging every possible input and variable. In his mind, he wanted solutions for the farmers of the South, not definitive proof for scientific journals.

"I never have to grope for methods," he once said. "The method is revealed at the moment I am inspired to create something new."[28]

His most useful experiments in this regard were with sweet potatoes and peanuts, both plentiful in the South. Peanuts, for example, were an ideal crop to grow in rotation with cotton, because peanuts returned the nitrates to the soil that cotton needed to flourish. At the time, however, peanuts were considered a garbage crop with few uses. If George could find real uses for the humble peanut, growing them in rotation with cotton would profit farmers. So he began his research with a simple prayer to God: "Why did you make the peanut? Why?"[29] He described what came next:

> With such knowledge as I had of chemistry and physics I set to work to take the peanut apart. I separated the water, the fats, the oils, the gums, the resins, sugars, starches, pectoses, pentoses, pentosans, legumen, lysin, the ameno, and amedo [sic] acids. There! I had the parts of the peanut all spread out before me. Then I merely went on to try different combinations of those parts, under different conditions of temperature, pressure, and so forth.[30]

Through his research over the years, George found 265 uses for the peanut, 118 uses for the sweet potato, and 85 for another plentiful crop from the South: pecans.[31]

They were far from an overnight success, however. An enormous obstacle remained to the success of Carver's inventions. The farming of peanuts as a cash crop was very difficult because foreign competition often kept prices low. When an import duty to give US growers a competitive edge was proposed in Congress, the House Ways and Means Committee conducted hearings on the matter.

On January 20, 1921, George was one of the witnesses, invited by the United Peanut Growers Association. The stakes were high. He knew he had a chance to make a huge difference in the economic prospects of so many people. Yet he must do it in a very short window of time, capturing the attention of suspicious congressmen. An ordinary man might have let his nerves overwhelm him. But Carver had a plan.

If the congressmen were expecting just another boring testimony, they were in for a surprise. George entered in his normal, unassuming way, wearing the same impeccable but slowly deteriorating suit he wore every day for most of his professional life. He freshened it up with a new flower in one of the buttonholes every day. Unlike other witnesses, he had a big box under his arm. He was about to demonstrate that more than just being a skilled scientist, he was also something else: a canny salesman.

Chairman Joseph W. Fordney, who very likely had never heard of Dr. George Washington Carver any more than the other members on the committee had, began the interview by admonishing him to limit his remarks to ten minutes.

George settled in. "Mr. Chairman, I have been asked by the United Peanut Growers' Association to tell you something about the possibilities of the peanut and its possible extension. . . . If I may have a little space here to put these things down, I should like to exhibit them to you."[32]

Several congressmen moved their chairs forward, leaning to see what he was producing.

"I am just going to just touch a few high places here and there because in 10 minutes you will tell me to stop," he said and theatrically removed an object from his chest. "This is the crushed cake, which has a great many possibilities . . . for flours and meals and breakfast foods. . . . And then we have the hulls, which are ground and made into a meal for burnishing tin plate." And on he continued.

As his ten minutes were coming to a close, one of the congressmen asked for an extension—probably out of curiosity about how many more things were in his box—and it was granted. George continued. Throughout the exchanges, he had the congressmen laughing and asking questions. Finally Chairman Fordney announced, "Go ahead, brother. Your time is unlimited."

Carver continued, "Here a short time ago, or some months ago, we found how to extract milk from peanuts. . . . Now, it is absolutely impossible to tell that milk from cow's milk in looks and general appearance. This is normal milk. The cream rises on it the same as on cow's milk, and in fact it has much of the same composition as cow's milk." He explained that it could be used as cream to make butter, ice cream, and more. "It makes the most delicious ice cream that I have ever eaten."

The congressmen began to grill him on objections to his tariff plan. He sparred ably, while taking time to continue demonstrating his products. Representative John Carew of New York broke in to ask about a popular fruity beverage: "How does it go in a punch?"

As if the question had been a setup, Carver replied, "Well, I will show you some punches."

Again laughter filled the chamber.

"Here is one with orange, and here is one with lemon, and here is one with cherry."

As more questions were put to him, he gave answers that sent the congressmen back into spasms of laughter. And so he went on until his box was emptied. Then he concluded, "If you go to the first chapter of Genesis, we can interpret very clearly, I think, what God intended when he said, 'Behold, I give you every herb that bears seed upon the face of the earth, and every tree bearing a seed. To you it shall be meat." That is what he means about it. It shall be meat. There is everything there to strengthen and nourish and keep the body alive and healthy."[33]

The committee received those remarks with another warm round of applause.

In response to other questions, he let them know he had been able to bring only about half of the items he had wanted to display. Representative Allen Treadway of Massachusetts answered that declaration with "Well, come again and bring the rest."

In all, George had been allowed an hour and forty minutes. Some weeks later, the committee promulgated the highest tariff on peanuts yet legislated at that time: three cents a pound on shelled nuts and four cents a pound on unshelled.[34] That protected the southern farmers from being undercut on prices from foreign peanut growers. It was likely that George's presentation had a strong influence on that decision.

Despite the wealth his research could have provided him, he took out only three patents on his discoveries, instead sharing his success generously with the world. For George Washington Carver, everything he taught came back to faith and Scripture:

> To those who have as yet not learned the secret of true happiness, which is the joy of coming into the closest relationship with the Maker and Preserver of all things: begin now to study the little things in your own door yard [backyard], going from the known to the nearest related unknown for indeed each new truth brings one nearer to God.[35]

It was a conviction he carried from his youth into a ripe old age. Along the way, the power of a peanut began with that now-familiar simple prayer to God: "Why did you make the peanut? Why?"

Remember the people who used to tease young George for his love of "the little things"? He said it was "considered foolishness." It's a good thing that he ignored them. If God dismissed little things, He wouldn't pay any attention to us! But Jesus says that the kingdom of Heaven is like a mustard seed growing into a mighty tree.

George overcame the tragedies and injustices of his childhood to become one of the most important scientists of the twentieth century (*Time* magazine later called him the "Black Leonardo"). His faith in God gave him the generous spirit to pour out blessings onto a war-devastated land. This is a story we see often in Scripture. The prophet Zechariah spoke powerfully to Israelite exiles returning to their ravaged homeland. He described the challenges to the Israelite leader, Zerubbabel, as if they were as big as a mountain. But then he said:

"What are you, mighty mountain? Before Zerubbabel you will become level ground. Then he will bring out the capstone amid shouts of 'God bless it! God bless it!' . . .

"Who dares despise the day of small things . . . will rejoice."

—ZECHARIAH 4:7, 10

Who dares despise the day of small things will rejoice. What an incredible promise. George Washington Carver's life is a reminder never to despise the little things. If you find yourself on what looks like barren ground, remember George's life and take another look. In the clay, in the mustard seed, even in the lowly peanut can lie God's purpose for your life that can change the world.

We all have moments that count as dark nights of the soul. How do we cope when fear and sadness have us in the grip? The world often defines strength as being tougher and harder than the next guy. But a Christian knows, like King David, that "The LORD is my strength and my shield; my heart trusts in him, and he helps me." (Psalm 28:7) The source of our hope, in our darkest moments, is our trust in God and our knowledge that He "will never leave you nor forsake you." (Deuteronomy 31:6) God promises restoration and reconciliation.

Restoration

"I will repay you for the years the locusts have
eaten. . . .
"You will have plenty to eat, until you are
full, and you will praise the name of the Lord
your God, who has worked wonders for you."

—Joel 2:25–26

THE SILENCE OF GOD

Even a pastor's faith can be tested beyond measure.

> My God, my God, why have you forsaken me?
> Why are you so far from saving me, so far from my
> cries of anguish?
>
> —PSALM 22:1

*P*astor Andrew Brunson stepped into the street. Behind him was Izmir Resurrection Church, a squat, cream-colored structure set between two taller buildings in Izmir, Turkey. It was just after a Friday prayer gathering, and Andrew was speaking with a parishioner from his church when an approaching man caught his eye.

The man was dressed in a camouflage jacket, and he was holding a gun. Andrew's attention zeroed in on the weapon, and the man's hand trembling violently on the dark grip of a pistol. Despite his shaking limbs, the man's face was set with furious determination.

Pop. Pop. Pop-pop-pop-pop.

The man's hand snapped back as he fired six shots in quick succession.

Andrew would later realize the gun was loaded with blanks. But then, realizing that the first gun was empty, the attacker dropped to one knee and pulled a shotgun from the bag he'd been carrying.

All Andrew could think of was the people inside the church and the damage the man could do to them. A massacre could be moments away. He sprang forward. From behind, he threw his arms around the assassin in a bear hug. The shotgun exploded into the air, the noise ringing in the narrow street. The attacker screamed, his voice taut with impotent fury, "We will kill you! You will give an account!"

The two men struggled, straining and elbowing, making Andrew's arms burn with effort. Andrew was numb. Lost in a haze of adrenaline, he believed that his life and the lives of his fellow Christians depended on his continuing to restrain the taller, stronger man.

And then . . . it was over. Policemen came dashing onto the street, grabbed the attacker's arms, and carried him away. Andrew retreated into the church. All the adrenaline hit him in one moment. He began shaking uncontrollably, overwhelmed with shock and relief. Despite everything, he realized, to his surprise, that he wasn't afraid.

The thing was, God had told Andrew so many times that He had a plan for him in Turkey. Now, trembling in the church he pastored, Andrew felt overwhelmed by God's faithfulness.

The attack at the church occurred in 2011, eighteen years into Andrew's life as a missionary. The son of American missionaries to Mexico, he had felt called to missionary work even before he had entered elementary school. One of his earliest memories was when he was three years old and his mother had introduced him to T. Stanley Soltau, a veteran missionary.

Many years before, as a young boy, Soltau had similarly been introduced to an elder missionary. In that case, it was Hudson Taylor, one of the very first Christian missionaries in China, who had journeyed deep into the mainland in 1853 at the age of twenty-one. Many years after Taylor had established himself as a legendary mission work organizer, Soltau's mother had taken her two young sons to ask Taylor to pray for them and to ask God to lead them into a life of missionary work.

Andrew Brunson's mother had done the same with Soltau. Andrew credits that moment with planting in him a desire, one he was too young to understand, to carry the Gospel to the world. Two generations of missionary calling descended onto the little boy's shoulders. Just like any little one, however, Andrew had been acting up. His mom spanked him. He later said that spanking "is what engraved the occasion in my mind and ensured I never forgot it."

Many years later, after meeting his future wife, Norine, at Wheaton College, Andrew turned the calling into a reality. Andrew and Norine moved to Turkey in 1993. They eventually put down roots in Izmir, a city of nearly 3 million people on the Aegean Sea. It must have been dizzying to set foot in a place with so much ancient and biblical history baked into its heritage. Izmir's urban history goes back 3,000 years, and its past as a human settlement dates back 8,500 years.

Izmir's original Greek name was Smyrna, which was also the name Jesus Christ used when He dictated a letter to the city's church in Revelation 2:8–10, comforting them in a time of persecution ("To the angel of the church in Smyrna write: . . . Do not be afraid of what you are about to suffer. I tell you, the devil will put some of you in prison to test you. . . . Be faithful, even to the point of death, and I will give you life as your victor's crown."). Other sites of biblical importance lie close by. Izmir has long been a center of trade, and Izmir Province incorporates many ancient cities. One of those is Ephesus, another recipient of a Revelations letter, the possible site where the Gospel of John was written, and the location of several fifth-century Christian councils. The Acts of the Apostles tells us that Saint Paul lived in Ephesus, working with a congregation and organizing missionary activity to spread the Good News of the Lord. It was from a prison in Rome that Paul wrote the Epistle to the Ephesians.

Despite its rich Christian history, Turkey has only a tiny Christian presence, with just .1 percent of the population identifying as Christian. Building a new church was an uphill battle, but in Izmir, the Brunsons established a small congregation, Izmir Resurrection Church, placing it in a transvestite red-light district. At first, they wondered if anyone seeking God would enter the zone. They needn't have worried; thousands of people moved through the area every day, passing the church.

Over time the members of the church came up with a strategy of leaving Christian books on the windowsills of the building. Before long, they were distributing more than a thousand New Testaments per month. Many people were just curious. Most had never met a Christian before, let alone visited a church. Some chose to convert. Many of them did so briefly, only to fall away after family and friends convinced them of the "error" of their ways. Some who came to the church simply wanted to stir up trouble. The Brunsons even discovered members who were secret police, there to keep an eye on this unlikely couple, self-described introverts, who had to put themselves out there in a very social, and potentially hostile, environment every day. The Brunsons were courageous because they believed God had chosen them and this mission in Turkey to prepare for a spiritual harvest.

Life was never dull. Andrew and Norine worked with refugees from war-torn Syria and Iraq, helping them by providing much-needed supplies—food and clothing mostly—to aid them as they sought to resettle their lives. The work was difficult yet rewarding.

Andrew was certain that staying in Turkey was a divine assignment. And so their family remained for twenty-three years. Andrew loved being an American, but accepted Turkey as his home.

But one day in 2016, Andrew felt God calling again. This time, the Lord was telling him to "come home." He wasn't sure what it meant, but it was disconcerting. He and his wife had bought a condominium, believing that they would live the rest of their lives in Izmir.

Five years had passed since the day Andrew fought the gunman at his church. He thought little of it when a request came for them to report to the local police station on October 7, 2016.

At the police station, Andrew and Norine learned that the Turkish government had issued an order to deport them from the country. They wondered if one of the troublemakers at the church had given the authorities some false accusation serious enough to cause them to have to be expelled from the country.

Andrew felt shocked that they were having their life's work seized from them. Andrew wondered whether maybe *this* was God's way of calling him home, even though he thought it seemed "contrary to everything we thought God had planned for us."

But their confinement dragged on. Norine was released after

thirteen days. Not Andrew. He had no idea what was about to happen.

This happened at the same time that Turkey exploded in unrest—teetering on the brink of an internal war.

Pastor Brunson was among a large group of people, including some Americans, who were arrested as part of a purge following the 2016 failed coup d'état attempt against the government and President Recep Tayyip Erdoğan. Two hundred and forty-one people had been killed and 2,194 others injured in the coup attempt, according to published reports.[36]

It was doubtful that the Turkish government seriously suspected Andrew was involved in a plot to overthrow the government. The other Americans held by Turkey were dual US-Turkish citizens, who the government may have perceived to have a right to be in the country. Andrew may have looked more like hostage material. "There were police files on me going back years," Andrew said. "This wasn't a mistake. I was the only one considered to be an American by the Turkish government, the only Christian, and the one they used to try to gain leverage with the U.S. government."

While some missionaries were being deported, Andrew was the only America detained for a long time. He suspects that someone high up said "let's hold onto him and see what happens." What began as a way to intimidate the local Christians turned into a negotiation with the US.

The physical circumstances for Andrew were dire—being locked up with nearly two dozen men in a cell designed for eight, often being denied visitation rights with his beloved wife, and having his future in the hands of a corrupt and unjust legal system. However, Andrew also experienced a spiritual challenge he had never anticipated.

FOR
Moments
WHEN YOU
NEED A
Prayer

Worship

God of all times and all places: you invite us to worship you through the beauty of the world around us, and in every experience of joy and love you give us. Open our hearts now to praise you for all these gifts. Fill our hearts to overflowing with gratitude, so that rivers of love pour out from us to everyone we meet. Bless our worship in spirit and in truth, and help us to hear your voice speaking to us today and every day. Amen.

(For scriptural inspiration, see Isaiah 6:1–10 and Psalm 118.)

Thanksgiving

Lord God, I give you thanks for all the blessings of this life: for the goodness that you reveal every day in the world around me, for your mercy to all those in need, and for your constant love that sustains the universe. Thank you for working all things together for my good. Most of all I thank you for the gift of your son, Jesus, whom you gave to redeem the world. Thank you for the hope of our heavenly calling, where we will one day live with you in joy past all telling. Amen.

(For scriptural inspiration, see 1 Timothy 4:4–5, Colossians 3:15, Romans 8:28, and Colossians 4:2.)

Lamenting

Lord Jesus, in your earthly life you knew what it was like to feel sorrow for those you loved, and you grieved for all who suffered. Help me now to understand my own grief and to know that you sit here with me, blessing my grief even as you have blessed my joys. Knowing that there is no comfort that the world can offer, I surrender to your loving arms. I trust that one day my own heartbreak will end in resurrection joy. And I ask that you hold me close until that day, in your infinite mercy and love that brings life to all things and a dawn to every dark night. Amen.

(For scriptural inspiration, see John 11:33–37.)

Peace

Lord God, you said to your apostles that the peace you would give them was not the peace of the world. But my heart aches for this world, as I know your own heart ached when you walked the earth. You see the brokenness of this world, and you grieve for all the victims of war, violence, and oppression, wherever they may be. Soften the hearts of all those who make war in the world, so that the peace of this earth may be a reflection of the peace of your heavenly kingdom. Make me an instrument of that peace, in my own family, in my work, and in my church. May your Holy Spirit wrap this earth in the mantle of your peace, that all may know and worship the Prince of peace. Amen.

(For scriptural inspiration, see Isaiah 11:6–9 and John 14:27.)

Family Togetherness

Lord God, from the beginning you created us to live together in families. By loving others, we come to understand your love more fully. Knit our family together in your grace, that we may bear one another's burdens, grieve one another's sorrows, and celebrate one another's joys. Above all else, fill us with compassion for one another, so that when we fail one another, we may remember your forgiveness and mercy toward each of us. May our family be a reflection of you that we may always be a shelter to those in need, a refuge for the brokenhearted, and a haven of peace to everyone we know. Bring our family at last to Heaven, where we may rejoice with you and with all the families of the earth, united in your worship and praise, forever and ever. Amen.

(For scriptural inspiration, see Psalm 127.)

Healing

Lord God, in your hand are all times and all seasons. You hold our souls in troubled times, and you comfort us in sickness. If it be your will, grant strength and health to my body as Jesus healed the sick who came to him. Grant me the wholeness of soul that will draw me closer to you, because there is no true health apart from your presence, and your love brings perfect strength. In all the workings of your will, may the Holy Spirit grant peace to my soul, come what may. Amen.

(For scriptural inspiration, see Isaiah 38:1–6 and Mark 10:46–52.)

Contrition

Lord Jesus, you forgave the woman weeping at your feet, and you called sinners to repentance and a new life. Like them, I have failed your love for me. I do love you, Lord, and I pray for the chance to show you my love. Even as I weep before you, I know that you have already put away all my sins, and like the father of the prodigal son, you embrace me and lift me up, holding me close. Forgive me, Lord God. Grant me the power of your Holy Spirit that I may not sin again. Thank you for the chance to serve you. May I never forget your mercy. May I show that same mercy to all those who have wronged or hurt me in any way. Amen.

(For scriptural inspiration, see 2 Samuel 12:1–13, Psalm 51, Matthew 6:12, and Luke 15:11-32.)

Meditation

Lord God and Father of all, help me to hear from you. Teach me to be still and know that you are God. Calm my mind so that I can hear you speaking to me. Quiet the rush of my thoughts and lead home the wanderings of my heart, that my soul may be steadfast and focused on you. Empty me, that I may be filled only with you. Make in me a home for your blessed son, Jesus. Amen.

(For scriptural inspiration, see Hebrews 1:1–2)

Adoration

Lord God, you are amazing and awesome. The planets in deepest space spin at your command, and your power upholds the fire of every star. But you are the same God who cares for each of your children here on Earth and who came to share this human life with us. Grant me the grace to love you more and more with every passing day, in mind, heart, and soul, until my body's last breath and beyond, if it be your will. May all your holy angels give you praise and worship, and may I join my voice to theirs in this life and the next. Amen.

(For scriptural inspiration, see Hebrews 1:3.)

Dedication for a Higher Purpose

Lord God, bless and consecrate me as I set out on this new road. Thank you for calling me to this holy purpose and this new state of life and for granting me the grace to hear your voice. May I be dedicated to the working of your will above all else, and may I have the courage and strength to serve you as the prophets did. Fill me, I pray, with your Holy Spirit now, that all fear may be banished and that I may be inspired in this calling by the fire of your love. May I always walk in your ways and bring glory to your holy name, from this day forth and forever. Amen.

(For scriptural inspiration, see Exodus 3:1–17, Exodus 15:20–21, 1 Samuel 3, and Jeremiah 1:4–10.)

Guidance

Lord God, you promised light to all those who seek your name and your truth. Send your light upon me now, because I cannot see the way. Be a lamp to my feet to light my path. While I am uncertain of my path, I trust in you. I know that you will never leave me nor forsake me. Drive away all fear and anxiety from my heart, and lead me step by step on the road that you would have me travel. Give me the courage to walk that road and the knowledge that Jesus walks beside me, no matter what awaits. Amen.

(For scriptural inspiration, see Deuteronomy 31:8, Psalm 119:105, and John 8:12.)

Pilgrimage

God of the journey, again and again in your holy word you called your people of faith to set forth on a road to greater understanding and deeper belief. You guided the footsteps of Naomi and Ruth as they sought a refuge in your holy land, and after your resurrection you walked with the disciples on the way to Emmaus. Reveal yourself now to me as you did to them, that I may make a pilgrimage to places which reignite my hunger for you, Lord. And cover me with your supernatural favor as I return home, safe and secure in your love. Amen.

(For scriptural inspiration, see Genesis 12:1–5, Ruth 1:7–22, and Luke 24:13–35.)

Children

Lord, guard my children's hearts and minds, so their actions never come from pride, anger, or bitterness. Help them reach out to you through prayer when they are tempted by the desire to do things out of selfish ambitions. With your love guiding my hand, I will teach them to imitate you, Lord. I pray you help them to walk in a spirit of kindness and gratitude. In Jesus' name, Amen.

(For scriptural inspiration, see Ephesians 4:31–32, Philippians 2:3–4.)

Intercession

Lord Jesus, on the night before you died you prayed to the Father for your disciples, asking that they would be strengthened and comforted in your absence. Hear my prayer now for all the ones I love. I pray especially for [prayer recipient's name] that your gracious will may be done and that your love and mercy be poured out upon [prayer recipient's name] richly. And, Holy Spirit, at times when I also have needed an intercessor, thank you for interceding for me with groanings too deep for words. In the power of your name I pray, Amen.

(For scriptural inspiration, see 1 Kings 17:17–24, John 17, Romans 8:26, and Acts 9:36–43.)

"My tests were enough to knock me out of my relationship with God," he said.

As time dragged on and he grew more and more isolated and depressed, he even began to question whether God existed. Even when he decided that God did exist, he felt deeply disappointed with Him, questioning whether God really was a good Father.

Andrew had read many biographies of Christians persecuted for their faith, but few had detailed the spiritual struggle they had gone through. That meant that he had gone into prison believing that the individuals who had gone before were extremely tough; that they had never broken; that they had remained shining examples of their faith. The fact that prison made him weaker and weaker made him feel like a failure. He felt like he had "broken," like he was "the weakest person in the world."

"My spiritual crisis with God was very significant," he said. "I thought I was pretty strong. But I had never counted the cost of being in prison. No one had been in prison for their faith in Turkey, at least not in living memory. I was disappointed and surprised that I broke so quickly."

Christians have struggled with "the silence of God" for many centuries. Job demanded, in the midst of his suffering, that God answer him, and eventually he received a response, though not the one he was expecting. Others weren't so lucky. King David, in Psalm 22:2, wrote, "My God, I cry out by day, but you do not answer, by night, but I find no rest."

In a song called "The Silence of God," Michael Card wrote, "It'll drive a man crazy/It'll break a man's faith/It's enough to make him wonder/If he's ever been sane." But in the same song he draws our attention to a statue of Jesus in Gethsemane, abandoned by His friends and praying an unanswered prayer: "My Father, if it is possible, may this cup be taken from me. Yet not as I will, but as you will." (Matthew 26:39) The Man of all Sorrows, Card implies, knew the silence of God, too. Jesus ultimately said the words of Psalm 22 on the cross, asking God why He had forsaken Him. Jesus knew and experienced silence, too.

It wasn't until after Andrew was released and he spoke with others who had endured similar circumstances that he learned that many people do break while in prison. It was actually the normal response. He knows that many people hesitated to be candid about their crisis of faith when recounting their persecution in memoirs. But it was important to Andrew that he be honest about what the ordeal was really like for him.

In retrospect, he does see God's grace sustaining him, even though he found it "mainly an unfelt grace" at the time. He now sees the first year of his imprisonment as one of breaking and the second as one of rebuilding. "I don't feel a sense of shame. I look back, and I see that actually I had many victories, and many of them were very small," he explained. "For example, a turning point for me was making the decision that I would turn my eyes toward God and not away from Him. If I'd gone by my emotions . . . well, they were in turmoil. They caused me to turn away from God and reject Him. I had to will myself to not do that. I had, each and every day, to choose to turn toward Him. That is a small thing, but it is a victory. Time after time, I had to make that choice, and I re-built my relationship with God and I survived that prison ordeal."

At the same time, he doesn't see his suffering as unique. "We're all tested in different ways, by different means," he said, "but the areas of the heart that are tested are the same. I think that we all, at some point, go through a crisis in our life when we feel the silence of God. We feel abandoned even though we're not. That sense of abandonment is a powerful emotion, and I clearly felt that way. And I wish that I had known ahead of time how difficult it could be. I had this idealized view of persecution. It would be difficult, but I would have a sense of God's presence. I didn't have that. Knowing what it would actually be like would have made me better able to deal with what I faced in prison."

For more than a year, he was held without being charged, but eventually he was charged with being a member of an armed terrorist organization, gathering state secrets for espionage, and attempting to overthrow the Turkish Parliament and government.

The case against Andrew was ludicrous. The Turkish state allowed secret witnesses to testify, a judge refused to allow his defense team to call witnesses, and the claimed web of entanglements with the various terror groups was insanely complex. One piece of "evidence" was that Andrew's daughter had sent him a photo of a regional rice dish that one of the terrorist groups frequently served in their safe houses.

Other "evidence" was based on sketchy witness testimony, GPS data showing that he was near the Syrian border (he had been there, but helping refugees), and a photograph showed him in that location speaking to a man who was wearing a yellow, red, and green scarf, the colors associated with Kurdish nationalists. In addition to that Andrew was accused of trying to Christianize the nation, that he was part of a "Mormon Gang" at work in the country, that his church was part of a CIA network linked to terrorists, and that he had been involved in brainwashing Turkish college students.

"When I was in prison, people would send me messages telling me to just trust God," Andrew said. "What they were saying is 'Andrew, trust God that He's going to get you out of prison.'

But the Bible doesn't say in any verse, 'Andrew is going to get out of prison.' And so I think when it comes to persecution, there are no guarantees. There are no guaranteed outcomes. God may intervene; He may not."

In Romans 8:28, Paul says, "We know that in all things God works for the good of those who love him, who have been called according to his purpose." But Andrew warns not to see that promise as an immediate solution to a problem. He said, "People in the West, especially Christians in the West, think, 'Well, I'm supposed to have a good outcome right now.' . . . God will turn [situations] for good, but I may not see the benefit very soon. I may not see it in this lifetime; I may only see it in eternity.

"The conclusion I came to is: We're human. We break, and God allows it. And He's still involved in that. And the challenge is to not become offended toward God, to not turn away from Him when we don't understand. In prison, with all of my questions and doubts, I chose to embrace Him, to continue running after Him, to continue turning my eyes toward Him, and say, 'I don't understand. But I still love you.' And that's what I'm encouraging people to do now, to say to God, 'I love you anyway. I will not turn away. I will still be faithful to you.'"

The international incident incited a diplomatic row between the United States and Turkey that was eventually resolved in a display of bureaucratic theater when Andrew was found guilty, sentenced to prison, released into an "appeals" process and immediately allowed to leave the country in October of 2018. This was really just the Turkish government saving face. US officials, including President Donald Trump, had been exerting pressure on the Turkish government.

When Andrew set foot on a US base as a free man, the

ambassador handed him a folded American flag. Andrew clutched it to his face. "I love my country."

Since his return to the United States, Andrew has had a lot of time to reflect on his experiences, and part of his "missionary" work has been to develop a series of talks about how to best deal with the obstacles that we all face in life. In one of those, he said, "I believe that there's going to be increasing hostility toward faithful followers of Jesus in this country. And so I'm trying to take from my experiences some things that could be transferable to others. I am urging people to prepare their hearts so that they are able to stand under pressure and remain faithful to God. I want to emphasize that this is not political. It's more saying: prepare yourself so that in difficult times, you will be able to maintain your faith in God.

"Because I loved God, I was willing to take risks for him, to invest my resources in His work, to suffer for Him. I love Jesus even more now because I suffered for Him. Love drives sacrifice. I came out of prison with a deeper intimacy with Him than I ever had before. I pursued God with unusual desperation because of the pressure I was under. I have never been so God centered in my life. Pressure pushes us to run after God in a way that we normally don't. I love this verse in Psalm 42, 'As the deer pants for streams of water, so my soul longs for you, O God. My soul thirsts for God, the living God.' What passion for God! But read the rest of the psalm. The psalmist is under tremendous pressure–surrounded by enemies, terribly discouraged, feeling forgotten by God. And so he cries out for God. Pressure makes us run after God as never before. And this is very good for us."

Pastor Andrew has also contextualized what he endured in this way: "The truth is that suffering builds perseverance, and this is so important to God that Paul tells us that we should even rejoice in our suffering for this reason. And James says, 'The testing of your faith develops perseverance. Allow perseverance to finish its work, so that you may be mature and complete, not lacking anything.'" (James 1:3–4)

As is true for all of us, our perspective on events changes over time. Pastor Andrew's being broken and feeling distant from God—and remaining faithful in spite of this—has had transformative effects on him that started a wave in his own life and has carried over into the lives of others as he continues ministering for God. He summed this process up best when he said, "Norine told me during some very dark times in prison, 'If we go through this the right way, at the end we will have no regrets.' When she said this, she didn't know whether I would gain my freedom in this life or not. She was pointing me to what really matters: be faithful, be obedient, run the race well. He is worthy, and He is worth it. As we look back now, I can say that we have no regrets. Of course, I know my race is not over yet, so I focus on running the race that is set before me now, to finish well, to be found worthy to stand before Jesus on that final day with no regrets. And I pray the same for you."

FINDING FORGIVENESS FOR
THE UNFORGIVABLE

A daughter praying for her mother hears from God.

> Jesus said, "Let the little children come to me, and
> do not hinder them, for the kingdom of heaven
> belongs to such as these."
>
> —MATTHEW 19:14

It was her mom's voice on the phone. "I've started attending a Bible study."

Nancy Owen* couldn't believe it. They were words she'd never thought she'd hear, words so totally at odds with the mother she knew, but words she'd prayed for. In a moment, she had hurtled back in time.

It was 1964. Kicked out of the house by her mom, ten-year-old

---

* For reasons of privacy, Nancy Owen is a pseudonym.

Nancy was navigating the busy streets at dusk, hoping that no one would molest her. She wasn't totally sure what that word meant, but she knew her mom wished it on her.

Through the years, young Nancy had weathered unthinkable threats before. Her intoxicated mother once had sped through hairpin turns on the northern California road while driving home from their grandma's house. "I think I'll just drive off the middle of the next curve into the lake and kill us all," her mom had threatened, repeating a death wish she'd made many times.

Why was her mother so focused on oblivion? Nancy simply couldn't understand.

Her older siblings had left an hour earlier. Being kicked out was a punishment handed down by a mother who preferred to lose herself in wine rather than engage with her children. Whenever the kids were forced out onto the street at night, the older ones would walk the thirty minutes to their dad's little grocery store, where they would stay with him until closing time. It wasn't much of a bedtime routine, but at least they were together.

Until that night, Nancy, the youngest of the three children, had been spared that penalty. She later attributed that mercy to God's blessing. But at the time, she isolated herself mentally. A key coping strategy was to bury herself in books: Nancy Drew, Trixie Belden, *Island of the Blue Dolphins*. "Books that were beyond my understanding," she said, and recalled one in particular, the story of a lost and lonely orphan. "*Jane Eyre*."

Nancy would surface from her fictional worlds only when her mom wanted more wine or needed someone to clean her vomit pan. Sometimes Nancy would hide physically as well. But not for the reason you might think. "Not hiding when she was drunk," she said. "More to see if anybody knew I was missing. I would hide near where people were. Almost never did anybody come looking for me."

Even as a child, she knew her home situation wasn't normal. She first realized it when she was five or six. Even earlier than that, hungry for affection, she would toddle across the street to play at a neighbor's house. The neighbor "was an amazing mom," she remembered. "I got that tender touch from her when I was there."

Things at home, though, remained dependent on her mother's mercurial depressive moods. So far, her mother hadn't driven any of her children into the lake. But that day in 1964, she seemed fully committed to the treacherous idea of turning her youngest child out into the streets at dark. "I'm going to make you leave, too, but I'm going to wait until it's dark," she'd snapped. "And I hope someone molests you on your way."

She had terrorized Nancy for two hours, constantly threatening that she would throw her out. As her mom's drunken tirade escalated to a crescendo, Nancy begged for relief: "Can I just go now?"

She wanted to leave the house while it was light outside. Still, she had to ask permission. From the bed where she lay, Nancy's mom wouldn't have known the difference, but despite everything, Nancy wanted desperately to please her mother. It didn't occur to her to just walk out or to go sit under a tree in their big backyard.

Just as the sun was setting and darkness was falling, her mom told her to get out of the house. "Don't you dare go to your father," she added.

But where else could she go? Traumatized and terrified, Nancy began traveling the longest distance her little legs had ever walked alone: along a busy street and across a bridge above the Russian River—the thirty-minute trek to her dad's store.

Finally, she arrived. Shelter. But obeying her mother, she didn't go inside. She huddled against the storefront on the ground. Sometimes she stood up to peek inside just so she could see her dad.

"Old men going in to buy wine stared at me," she said. She thought about the word *molest* and wondered if her mom would get her wish.

After several hours, her mom came marching around the corner, her cadence brisk and face livid. "I didn't go in! I didn't go in!" Nancy exclaimed, desperately afraid of upsetting her mom further. Her mom stormed into the store. Nancy watched through the window as her mom's body language morphed from rigid fury to wracking sobs and semihysteria. She could hear her mother's voice, and the panic and anger sounded genuine.

"The kids left, and I didn't know where they were," she told her husband. Perhaps, her stupor waning, she had become truly concerned. Nancy remembered feeling as though she was in big trouble but knowing her dad would protect her.

And he did. Once he realized what had happened, Nancy's dad ran out of the storefront, scooped his daughter into the safety of his arms, and sent his wife home. Father and daughter closed the store and walked home together at midnight. The older siblings had not come to the store, so the evening ended with Nancy falling asleep in the back of their old Rambler station wagon while her dad drove for hours, looking for her brothers and sister.

Everyone had school and work the next morning.

NANCY HAS ALWAYS LOVED CHILDREN. Now sixty-eight, she spent many years of her career teaching kindergarten. "I love the innocence of kids, that delightful air of being a child and finding your imagination." That innocence and imagination are things she feels tasked to protect, since she struggled so much to find them herself.

She knew Jesus, starting in middle school, though only by name. "I had a piano teacher who was talking to me about Jesus," she said. "Somehow I always knew He was there. I didn't know I could know Him personally, but He was wonderful."

Growing up in Ukiah, California, a quiet logging community close to the redwoods, Nancy and her siblings did have good days. When she wasn't drinking, Nancy's mom would take the kids to the river to swim, sometimes getting in to splash and play with them. On carefree days, Nancy would walk to the grocery store, exchange a soda pop can for a nickel, and promptly buy a five-cent candy bar.

But the alcohol made life unpredictable and treacherous. Would their mom call the school again while drunk or volunteer for the PTA? Would she swim in the river or threaten to drive her kids into it?

Not long after the incident when Nancy was thrown out, their father moved the family to a house two blocks from his store. He tried everything to help his wife, including taking her to a psychologist. After three appointments, she refused to go. Seeing no path for improvement, Nancy's dad filed for divorce.

Then things changed.

Nancy's not sure of the exact moment, but at some point, she realized she wasn't living in fear anymore. She hardly knew what life was like without that all-encompassing dread. During the years after the divorce, Nancy's life expanded beyond the confining walls of alcoholism and abuse.

At seventeen, she accepted Jesus into her heart. It was a major step in her journey toward healing. A big hurdle for her to clear was accepting that she was worthy of love at all. "We did go to church on Easter Sunday, I just didn't know what that had to do with me," she admitted. "I believed God had a relationship with people, but I thought you had to be a special person. I didn't feel special as a kid. If God's looking out over the universe and He says, 'I'll take these five' . . . I was in the background in the back of the audience."

In a way, both Nancy and her mother owed their darker feelings to childhood trauma, as Nancy eventually learned. One day toward the end of Nancy's high school years, her father told her why her mom drank so much: their first child, born a year after they had gotten married, died within hours of birth. Her mom was just fourteen years old, at the time.

"Mom got married when my dad was seventeen and she was thirteen. They went to Reno, Nevada, and lied about her age," Nancy said. "He told me she got married to get away from home."

Not long after Nancy's mom fled her own home, she was pregnant. Nancy's heart broke when she learned the story of her mother's tragedy. "The doctor came and stood at the door—he didn't even come into the room—and said, 'Your baby just died. If the nurses had let me know sooner, I could have saved him.' Then he walked out and left her all by herself."

While most fourteen-year-old bobby-soxers were swooning over Frank Sinatra, Nancy's mom was lying in a hospital room alone, unable even to hold her dead child. She was still just a child herself. She had never had a drink before that day.

WHEN NANCY WAS A SOPHOMORE in college, she got a call that her mom was in the hospital. She had swerved into an oncoming car, injuring another mom and her two daughters. There was no intersection and no reason to turn where she did, other than an oncoming car's potential to erase a life spent in pain. She was still looking for oblivion.

The people in the other car survived, although the littlest girl had critical injuries. Nancy's mom had a 50 percent chance of survival. *So*, Nancy thought, *she finally did it. She finally made good on her broken-record threat to try to kill herself on the road.*

Tears streaming down her face, Nancy sat in a heap on the floor of the hallway outside her mother's door, pleading with God to let her mother live. As a new Christian, all she wanted was for her mom to experience the same life and joy which she had. "God, please heal my mom and let her live," she prayed. "Let her live long enough to know Jesus as her Savior."

Two days later, Nancy overheard the doctors talking at the nurses' station. "It's a miracle," one of them said. "None of us thought she'd live through the first night." Six weeks later, her mom left the hospital.

God had answered the first part of Nancy's prayer: her mom's life had been saved. But Nancy wanted her mom to experience healing and peace. She kept praying. She talked with her mom about God whenever they got together, but the promise of something deeper than mere physical renewal seemed to be beyond her mom's grasp.

It was as though her mom, who had once taught her kids that the way to get to Heaven was to do more good things than bad, knew that under that strict system she didn't have a chance. Like Nancy, she didn't think herself worthy of love. Nancy had buried herself in books and learning. Her mother buried herself by drinking away the night with her second husband at the local Moose Club. But like her daughter, she was being drawn, slowly, by God's grace.

Five years after Nancy's bedside vigil, she got a call from her mom. Her mouth dropped when she heard what her mom had to say: she had joined a Bible study group and was loving the weekly reading and homework. "Over the coming months, whenever we talked on the phone, there was life and joy in her voice," Nancy said.

Before long, her mother began ordering soft drinks at the Moose Lodge instead of alcohol. She became an amazing grandmother to Nancy's children, who loved the fishing excursions and whimsical adventures she planned for them. Watching the relationship blossom between her now-sober mother and her children, Nancy caught a glimpse of the mother she'd always longed for but had never had. Instead of adding to her hurt, it fueled her feelings of gratitude for what God had done in her mother's life.

Key to her sense of acceptance was that Nancy had come to see God as a protector. Though she struggles even now, she says she faces such moments by intentionally focusing "on God and the ways He has answered prayer and taken care of me in the past. And remembering who He is."

Does He answer prayers every time? No. But "there have been *enough* times where He has answered prayer, [even though] He doesn't always answer the way we want."

Nancy and her mother never discussed the dark contours of the past, though they came close one time. "I really don't think that she did realize how she treated us," Nancy said. "It never came up, even after she knew the Lord."

But there was one prayer request that remained ungranted. Years after Nancy's mom had driven her car into the path of an approaching car, Nancy found herself sitting at a hospital bedside again, surveying her mother's face and thinking back over the rocky terrain of their story. Now, a new tragedy . . . a heart attack. Her mom was in a coma and it did not look good. "God, please heal my mom and let her live," Nancy said the same prayer she had reached out with years earlier. Again, she kept a round the clock vigil.

She turned to a book that had comforted her for twenty years, the Bible. "While I was reading, I came across the story where Isaiah told Hezekiah that he was going to die, but Hezekiah prayed and begged for more life and God said, 'I'll give you fifteen years.'" Something stirred in her spirit, and she knew those words were for her. She looked at her mom. She did the math. It had been exactly fifteen years since her mom had tried to take her own life. "I knew it was time to let her go," Nancy said.

Her mom died two days later.

CHILDHOOD TRAUMA IS TRICKY. IT reaches out and grabs you whether you're ready to deal with it or not. Once, when her daughter was leaving for a mission trip, only a few hours away, Nancy found herself experiencing extreme anxiety about it. Once God revealed to her that that was stemming from her unprocessed fears from her youth, she was able to offer it up to Him in prayer.

Nancy's mom died in 1989. Today, Nancy says God has completely healed her childhood trauma. But it took years. And then suddenly she was blessed, cleansed of the pain of her past. Shortly before Nancy's fiftieth birthday, God purged a memory that had plagued her throughout her life. "When I was six or seven, my mom told me that when she was pregnant with me, they couldn't afford another child, so she convinced herself that I was a tumor. She started calling me her little tumor," Nancy said. "To me that was total rejection. That story—and profound feelings of rejection—haunted me for decades."

Yet God's healing came in an instant. While attending a small prayer retreat more than a decade after her mom had died, Nancy shared that story with another woman at the retreat.

"I'm going to put my hand here by your chest, and I'm going to pray that memory and that label out," the woman told Nancy. After that prayer, the sting of rejection was gone.

"I'd felt that horrible feeling for decades. And after that prayer, I went back to my seat knowing deep in my spirit that—as best she could—my mom had always loved me," Nancy said.

Stories of loves can be complicated. Nancy says she understands better than ever that her mom—broken and traumatized—did the best she could to cope in an era that didn't understand grief recovery after the loss of a child. She is grateful that God extended her mom's life, giving Nancy a chance to experience her mother's healing and transformation. Most of all, she continues to rejoice that God isn't done with any of us yet—and that His passion to redeem and heal our trauma is ongoing in all of our lives.

"When I accepted the Lord, He began to deal with the fear in my life," she said. "It felt foreign. I got used to living with fear."

The fear ebbed slowly, like a receding tide. "Little things over time," she explained. "I would be afraid of something. The next time it happened there was less fear."

She described their house, perched above Coos Bay in Oregon. Gradually, the ground underneath it had eroded, and a torrential rainy season—unusually brutal even for Oregon—had made things worse. The earth on top of the bedrock had begun to slide. People at school had been praying for her family.

But, she said, "I remember standing at the copy machine one day and someone said, 'Nancy, how's your house?' I literally had to stop and think a minute, 'What's wrong with my house?' There was such peace that God was going to take care of us."

She speaks about winter storms now with great fondness. They're something happening outside, while we're within, safe and cozy.

Now she says that her childhood trauma forged inner strength, though in the opposite way that the world thinks of strength. Instead, it taught her to depend on God in all circumstances. Her life is also a startling testimony of the possibility of healing. Trauma is beatable.

"Never give up," she said. "God transcends everything we think gets in the way of healing. Even if the circumstances don't look pleasant, I *know* that I *know* that I *know* that God is with me. He will walk with me and carry me through anything."

ONE NIGHT IN AURORA

Evil versus peace, love, and a mom who knows the Lord

> Do not be overcome by evil, but overcome evil
> with good.
>
> —ROMANS 12:21

There were a loud pop and a trail of smoke. The sizzling sound of something flying through the air. More popping sounds and bright flashes in the darkness. The aroma of buttered popcorn overtaken by a chemical smell. Muffled coughs suddenly turned into shrieks of terror.

MARIE ISOM'S DAUGHTERS, MICHELLE AND Elizabeth, ages sixteen and fourteen, started screaming. "What's going on, Mom? What's happening?"

Marie and her girls were at a midnight showing of *The Dark Knight Rises*, the highly anticipated third installment of the Batman movie trilogy.

Marie was not particularly a fan of superhero or action movies, and she certainly wasn't a fan of midnight screenings. But she was a fan of spending time with her kids. She knew that parents sometimes make sacrifices for kids who are desperate to see a movie on opening night—even when opening night stretches into early morning.

In a matter of seconds, Theater 9 at the Century 16 multiplex in Aurora, Colorado, was a maelstrom of panic and confusion. The place was packed and some of the excited moviegoers were even dressed as characters from the Batman movies so a masked figure dressed all in black didn't really stand out.

Marie didn't notice the young man depart the theater about twenty minutes into the movie, and she certainly didn't know he had propped open an emergency exit while he changed into tactical gear and grabbed weapons from his car parked directly behind the building.

When the man reentered the crowded theater and started firing, Marie, like many others in the audience, thought it was some sort of special-effects spectacle, part of celebrating the popular film. Maybe someone is lighting off fireworks? she wondered. Disoriented at first, she felt momentarily paralyzed.

Her daughters' screams broke the spell. "I looked around and saw a dark figure," she recalled, "about forty or fifty feet straight ahead of us. He had a gun." That was when she finally found her voice. "Get down!" she screamed to her girls. "Get down!" And that was when she began to pray.

WHY WAS SHE EVEN HERE, in this theater, at this ungodly hour? Marie preferred to watch movies at home, where the benefits included closed captions and foot rubs by her husband, Scott. She was rejecting that emotional pull to make her girls happy and spend time with her babies who were growing up so fast.

Michelle and Elizabeth had been talking about that particular showing for months. At first their older, married sister had planned to go with them, but she'd recently become pregnant and was too sick and too tired to accompany them. That was when Marie reluctantly stepped in.

Then came an offer, a reprieve. Her eighteen-year-old son had also purchased tickets for the same multiplex. Planning to attend with friends, he offered to drive his younger sisters. Already feeling tired, Marie was tempted to skip the movie. "They would be watching the same movie, but in the next theater over, in the same building," she recalled. "It seemed like a good idea, but something kept telling me, 'Just go. Go with your girls.' So I did and will be eternally grateful I heeded that still, small voice."

WITH THEATER 9 NEARLY FILLED to capacity when they arrived, Marie somehow spotted five open seats six or seven rows up. She took a seat between Michelle and Elizabeth, the three of them sitting at the end of the aisle.

Right before the movie started, a couple arrived and asked if the pair of seats next to them was available. Marie and the girls figured they would simply slide over. But before they could move, the couple sidled past and took the two open seats.

Shortly after midnight on July 20, 2012, the theater lights dimmed and the projector flashed images on the big screen. Head in hand, Marie yawned.

TWO OF THE THREE ISOM women dropped facefirst onto the dirty floor. The youngest was seemingly frozen in place, so Marie yanked her to the ground and behind the row of seats.

They were surrounded by the sound of gunfire, the sounds of terror, the sounds of desperate survival. The gunshots were, according to Marie, "rapid and nonstop," the soundtrack of a massacre.

"Suddenly it dawned on me that my youngest daughter, Elizabeth, was straight down the aisle from the gunman," Marie said. "If he walked forward and began shooting, she would take a direct hit. I threw myself over her and hoped my tiny frame would be enough of a shield to save her life if a bullet struck. To say the least, at that moment I was freaking out."

Draped over her daughter, Marie continued to pray. Barely a whisper, barely formed words, she prayed the best she could in a frenzied moment—for safety, for God's presence, for the shooting to end. "It was more of a groaning than a spoken prayer," she recalled. "I sought God's peace and protection for those in the theater, for the carnage, for the nightmare to stop. I prayed that my kids would be okay if I died."

In fact, Marie thought she was going to die. And that was when she felt it—an unexpected sense of peace that fell upon her. "I did not fear death," she recalled. "Me—a girl who had spent a lifetime cowering in fear—wasn't afraid to die. That peace was a supernatural gift. I didn't want to die, and I didn't want to suffer pain, but I would be okay if I did. That thought, and that peace, gave me strength to keep praying."

When there was a momentary break in the shooting, people inside the theater began a mad dash for the exits. "At one point I momentarily lost sight of Michelle," Marie said. "I screamed her name and felt flooded with relief when I saw her. I had Elizabeth by the hand and was pulling her along with me."

The trio ran out of the theater and into the night. They followed the surging masses to the parking lot, caught in the swell of the crowd pushing them forward. Marie described the scene in her blog, in a post written later that same day. She still hadn't slept yet when she recalled how she and her daughters had leapt to their feet and joined the fleeing masses:

> We had to step over a lifeless body, people were screaming and pushing, not knowing where the shooter was. We raced to our car and I dumped my purse, frantically searching for keys, looking all around, prepared to hit the ground. I yelled at Michelle to call her brother Matthew and find out if he had made it out of the theater next door. She did. He did. We booked on out of there.

Marie recalled seeing bloodied people running and limping. Somewhere along the way, she lost one of her new Croc sandals and sprinted lopsided. "I'm not sure why I didn't kick the other one off," she said. "I felt the cold floor under my bare foot and later the cement, but I barely processed these things. I had one goal in mind: get my girls safely to the car and make sure that Matthew and his friends were safe."

It turned out that some bullets from Theater 9 actually made it to the adjoining theater, the one where Matthew was watching another showing with his friends. Three people in the other screening were injured. "It was sad that people in the next theater were injured," Marie reflected. "But it was nothing like the massacre taking place in Theater 9."

That massacre would set Marie on a new trajectory, with a new outlook on life and faith.

BORN IN VERMONT IN THE 1960s, Marie remembers growing up in a dysfunctional family. Both of her parents drank a lot, and each had a troubled childhood that they carried into their marriage. Her mom and dad divorced when Marie was in the fourth grade.

"In my childhood homes, there was a lot of drinking, fighting, and traumatic moments for a child," she recalled. "And lots of chaos. Lots of strangers—strangers to me—staying overnight. One man spoke very explicitly to me. . . . He told me what boys would want to do to me. He often talked dirty to me. I was just stepping into my teen years, so I didn't know what to do about it."

That unhealthy environment and the unpredictability of her home life prompted a need in Marie to control her world; more specifically, to overcontrol her situation and surroundings. She adopted the belief that if she were somehow good enough, diligent enough, and intentional enough, she could control and protect herself and her family.

Marie says she used to go to bed each night worried and fearful about what might happen with her kids, her extended family, her job, and every other aspect of her life. By the time of the shooting, however, she had already come a long way in overcoming what she calls skewed ideas and unhealthy beliefs. Her growing faith in God was a significant part of her recovery, and that night in Theater 9 was yet another step along the way.

"I was in my forties when the shooting occurred," she recalled. "I had already worked through many of the issues from my upbringing and acknowledged that trying to control every aspect of my life was an illusion. The shooting was another part of the journey to the freedom found in surrendering it all to God, of letting go of the idea that if I could protect my children from evil or hurt, I could control their environments."

THE POLICE CAPTURED THE GUNMAN, twenty-four-year-old James Holmes, behind the theater. He was standing by his car and didn't resist. But the damage he had inflicted was immense: he was later found guilty of murdering twelve people and wounding seventy others.

Her husband didn't immediately understand the tragedy his family members had just experienced. At that time, Scott worked an early-morning shift, so Marie and her daughters ended up waking him just a few hours before he was headed to work. One of the girls phoned him on their way home from the theater. "She was whimpering and trying to explain, saying 'But we're okay, we're okay,'" Marie said. "He really had no idea what was going on. It wouldn't be until much later in the day, with all the news coverage, that he really came to understand just how traumatic the night had been."

Marie and her children were still in shock the day after the shooting. They escaped the theater unharmed but not unscathed. Marie learned later that one of the fallen was the woman who had sat next to her older daughter in the theater. "Had we moved down," she explained, "Michelle would have been in the seat of a woman who was killed."

Experiencing moments of panic, Marie struggled to absorb all that had happened. "At one point," she recalled, "I asked my son, who had been in the military and had seen a lot of carnage, to go look for a bomb under our car. Because we didn't yet know anything about the shooter—if he worked alone or what—I decided that he might have planted explosives under cars in the parking lot." Traumatic experiences often cause people to become hyper-vigilant, and that was the case with Marie.

Through the painful days and weeks ahead, God served as her rock and anchor, the one sure thing in her life when everything else was falling to pieces. As time passed and healing slowly began, Marie alternately gave thanks for being alive and prayed that she would not waste the gift she had been given.

Sometimes, however, she wasn't sure quite how to pray. "I was upset that people were blaming God when I knew that God is not the author of evil," she said. "It was the choices of a man that caused so much bloodshed and heartbreak. I felt guilty for being alive when so many young people had died. I prayed for healing for my girls—that they wouldn't be dominated by fear. I had a strong faith, but they didn't. I also prayed that God would bring something good from the tragedy."

IN HER BLOG POST PUBLISHED eighteen hours after the shooting, titled "So You Still Think God Is a Merciful God?", Marie affirmed that God is not the cause of evil but rather the one who brings comfort and peace in the midst of it. Her conclusion: "God is always good. Man is not. Don't get the two confused."

She concluded her post by requesting prayers for the families who had lost loved ones and for those, particularly the young people, who had witnessed the horrors in Theater 9. Though Marie said she was still in shock when she wrote it, her post eventually garnered more than a million views. "That floored me," she says, "because I had been writing for an audience of something like seven followers and a few Facebook friends. Pastors were using my post in their Sunday services. People all over the world started messaging me and sharing how God had used the post to grow their faith. . . . That, to me, was an answer to my prayer to be used by Him."

Marie understands, however, that not everyone comes through tragedy with a positive outlook. Unanswered prayers, she says, can be extremely difficult to understand. Why do innocent people die? Why do natural disasters destroy entire communities? "I can't answer all of that," she said, "but I know the one who holds the answers—the one who brings peace and comfort in the midst of devastation."

Marie trusts that one day it will all make sense. But today is not that day. So she will cling to her faith and to prayer, because that is what she knows. "I will keep praying, because no matter how He answers or doesn't answer, I have tasted the goodness of God," she said. "There is no one else I would rather go to with my struggles and celebrations, knowing that He covers me with His love."

She knows she has come a long way since her childhood. There is deep peace, Marie said, in accepting that she has no control over anyone else's choices. She can offer advice or counsel to those who ask, but mostly she concentrates on loving others unconditionally.

After all, she understands full well that things could have turned out far differently for her family. Marie thought she was about to die that night at the theater, yet God covered her with peace as she prayed, even as shots rang out all around her.

"I don't believe in happily-ever-after endings and everything being neat and tidy," she said. "But I have discovered that, no matter what, every day is filled with beauty and joy."

Today, Marie reflects on the tragedy she endured and says,

"Because I had already held on to my faith through so many other difficult times in life—and had seen God move mountains—by the time this tragedy happened, my faith was established enough to know that He would bring me through it."

Marie's faith—and God's power—did indeed carry her through to a place of healing and wholeness.

Sometimes just getting started can be the hardest part of our faith walk. Prayer is more than just wishful thinking. It's discipline. It's warfare. It's how we fight back against the darkness. And prayer takes hard work. We must dedicate ourselves to reading and knowing the scriptures. And we mustn't quit.

"Everyone who competes in the games goes into strict training," Paul wrote in 1 Corinthians 9:25. "They do it to get a crown that will not last, but we do it to get a crown that will last forever." Our training is spiritual, but it should be as rigorous as that of an athlete competing for an earthly crown.

Perseverance

REES HOWELLS AND THE PRAYER WARRIORS OF DUNKIRK

Nothing affects history like fervent, persistent prayer.

> Rejoice always, pray continually, give thanks in
> all circumstances; for this is God's will for you in
> Christ Jesus.
>
> —1 THESSALONIANS 5:16–18

H"ave you been born again?"

Silly question, Rees Howells thought, helping his cousin Evan Lewis push coal into a bucket. The two men were deep down in a mine, and Evan seemed to suddenly be thinking about the stuff of Heaven and not the very real stuff of Earth coating their hands and faces.

"What do you mean?" Rees snapped defensively. "My life is as good as yours."

Despite Evan's attempt to explain what he meant, Rees couldn't grasp it. He scoffed at his cousin and went back to work.

What sort of question is that? he thought. *I never miss prayer meeting.* But the more Rees thought about it, the more uneasy he felt. He felt sick to his stomach when he remembered the verse the preacher had read the day he had left his home in Wales to go work in the United States: "Since we are surrounded by such a great cloud of witnesses, let us throw off everything that hinders and the sin that so easily entangles." (Hebrews 12:1) In his mind's eye, he pictured generations of his family, clouds of saints in the scriptures, looking at his life, at his grimy hands and grimier soul, and judging them wanting. Still, all he told his cousin as they walked down the road to town was "I am a Christian, and that's good enough for me."

But he remained uneasy. In fact, he was so uneasy that he packed his bags and fled one hundred miles away from the mine, from his cousin Evan, and, most important, from uncomfortable questions.

It was no good. God kept tugging at Rees's heart. The young Welshman felt paralyzed with fear, but didn't know how to resolve it. So he made a deal with the Almighty. He told people at the time, "If you show me an individual who is truly living the Sermon on the Mount, I will give in."[37]

The deal gave him some leeway. He could look around and say, 'Well, that man may seem devout, but has he truly given up everything for God?' It was safe to assume he'd never find someone who really believed all that Jesus said in the Gospels about giving your everything for the Lord. He kept coming back to the words he'd told his cousin: my life is as good as yours. It seemed a safe bet that he'd never find anyone with a truly better life than a man who never missed prayer meeting.

It was no safe bet. Not long afterward, Rees met Maurice Reuben, a wealthy man who had converted to Christianity despite knowing such a choice would lead to his disinheritance (Reuben's father's will proscribed any change of religion). Reuben's fervor had led his family to briefly have him committed for insanity. He had been released only after the judge had pointed out that if we were to imprison people for hearing the voice of God, we'd have to imprison the Apostle Paul. Now Reuben traveled the country, speaking for Jesus.[38]

Rees was stunned by the man's devotion. Many years later, his son would say in an interview, "When Father heard that testimony he was really broken. . . . And the Lord asked him, 'Is this your man?' And he said, 'Yes.' His life changed completely."[39]

Little did Rees Howells know, but he would become a mighty prayer warrior himself, leading a battle on one of the most important battlefields of the twentieth century: an invisible battlefield.

As German chancellor Adolf Hitler prepared for war in the late 1930s, so did a small Bible college in Wales run by Rees, who had returned to the land of his birth. Whereas the Nazis' mobilization consisted of endless drilling, seizing and repurposing factories to create weapons, imprisoning political enemies, and gobbling up small countries one by one, the members of the Bible College of Wales was doing something far more powerful: they were storming the fortress of Heaven with their prayers.

The Welsh theologian Martyn Lloyd-Jones once wrote, "Prayer is beyond any question the highest activity of the human soul. Man is at his greatest and highest when upon his knees he comes face to face with God."[40]

Rees believed that, too. During the war, he wrote, "I want to know that the Holy Spirit is stronger than the devil in the Nazi system. This is the battle of the ages, and victory here means victory for millions of people."

Many historians are puzzled by the bizarre decisions Hitler made throughout the war that eventually cost him victory. But few know that behind many of the decisions was a band of prayer "soldiers" who prayed, "Lord, bend Hitler" throughout the war.[41] As they did so again and again, Hitler made uncharacteristic and imprudent choices that gave his opponents time to prepare, cost him strategic opportunities, and eventually turned the tide of the war.

Rees was an unlikely college president. The sixth of eleven children, he had followed his father into the coal mines when he was twelve, starting as many did who spent their entire lives working in those dangerous and unhealthy conditions. Many of the rugged green mountains of Wales were riddled with mines. For many Welshmen, coal mining was the industry of their fathers and what they expected to work at their entire lives. Rees Howells, however, returned to Wales, only to be swept up in a revival led by the Welsh evangelist Evan Roberts in 1904–1905 and the calling to ministry, which he sensed changed everything. He founded a local mission, adding an extra three hours to each day to work there in addition to his regular shifts in the mines.

It took Rees a while to conceive of the Holy Spirit not just as a force but as a person, equal with God. Rees's son, Samuel, said that when his father finally accepted that, he wrestled with the implications. "The Lord showed him clearly that it meant a full and complete surrender. If he were to accept the Holy Spirit as a person, then he would not be living, but the Spirit. 'You go out, and I'll come in.' That was the challenge. It took him some days of deep dealing . . . [before] he knew that [the Spirit] had entered him as a person. . . . That was the changing point in his whole life."[42]

What Samuel was referencing was how, once we have accepted Jesus, God sends the Holy Spirit to be our guide and teacher. (John 14:16–17) He was probably also alluding to Galatians 2:20, which explains how Christ lives in us.

This is more than just a change in mindset. Rather, accepting it leads to us discarding the person we were before for a new one—replacing a dead existence with a living one. Paul wrote in Ephesians, "You were taught, with regard to your former way of life, to put off your old self, which is being corrupted by its deceitful desires; to be made new in the attitude of your minds; and to put on the new self, created to be like God in true righteousness and holiness." (Ephesians 4:22–24)

Accepting the Spirit of God means that we are transformed. We're no longer at the mercy of our passions and appetites, because the Spirit changes our minds and hearts so that we can become (and *want* to become) more and more like Jesus every day. The Spirit brings us into greater joy and purpose than we have ever known, as we become both more Christ-like and more fully ourselves than we ever were when we were governed by sin.

The mission's success led to Rees and his wife relocating to South Africa as missionaries, where they were part of several revivals. Then, in 1920, Rees felt called to return to Wales and establish a Bible college, God telling him to buy an estate called Glynderwen for their campus when he only had two shillings to his name.

Rees was no fundraiser, either. After reading an autobiography by the German-born English evangelist and educator George Müller, he determined that he would ask no one for money but God in prayer, just as Mr. Müller had for the orphanages he felt

God had called him to build. Rees never veered from that vow, and the last £140 of £5,800 needed arrived in the morning post just before he signed the contract to take possession of Glynderwen.

By the time the Nazis were threatening the rest of Europe in 1938, the Bible College of Wales had purchased three estates for its campus and ministry endeavors. At the time, Great Britain was woefully unprepared for war in the face of Germany's growing military might. The Nazis had already annexed Austria and had moved to do the same in the Sudetenland, part of Czechoslovakia. While war seemed imminent, rather than turning to invade elsewhere, Hitler signed the Munich Agreement on September 30, postponing the war with the rest of Europe for almost a year. In the weeks prior to the signing of that agreement, Rees and those in his Bible college dedicated themselves to prayer with the same commitment and tenacity as a soldier on the battlefield. Seeing the threat the Nazi movement posed to the rest of the world, Rees led his faculty and students to pray regularly for events to turn, even suspending classes to do so.

"We are on slippery ground," he told his students. "Only intercession will avail. God is calling for intercessors—men and women who will lay their lives on the altar to fight the devil, as readily as they would have to fight the enemy on the Western Front."[43]

One hundred twenty teachers and students heard Rees's words that day and agreed that they would join in fervent prayer until victory was won. It was in the weeks before the signing of the Munich Agreement that they first petitioned God with the words "Lord, bend Hitler."

Though many people look at the Munich Agreement as a failure on the part of British prime minister Neville Chamberlain and others to recognize that Germany would not be appeased, the pact gave the Allies time to prepare before Germany invaded Poland in September 1939 and Great Britain and France were forced to declare war on Germany. According to Sir Nevile Henderson, the British ambassador to Germany at the time of the agreement:

> "You are the only man," [Hitler] said somewhat bitterly to Mr. Chamberlain, "to whom I have ever made a concession." . . .
>
> Hitler felt irritated with himself. A section of his followers were always egging him on to fight England while the latter was still militarily unprepared. They reproached him for having accepted the Munich settlement and thus having missed the most favourable opportunity. An uneasy feeling lest they might have been right contributed to Hitler's ill humour.[44]

That same month, Italy announced that all Jewish people must leave the country in six months' time. That, together with the rising anti-Semitism in Nazi Germany, prompted Rees to become even more supportive of the Jews. His fervor gained intensity as Hitler started "throwing out" Jewish children along the Polish border a few weeks later.

Rees began looking to buy property to purchase to make a home for as many of the displaced Jewish children as he could. He ended up offering more than twice as much for a fourth estate as they had for any of the previous, some £20,000, though the school had nothing in the bank to repay the loan. At one point, school leaders even planned to sell the first three estates to raise £100,000 to give on behalf of the Jews. However, when the war erupted after the invasion of Poland, all of these decisions were put on hold. All the same, the burden to pray for the Jews stayed with Rees and his students throughout the war and into the years that followed.

By the time the Nazis invaded France in May 1940, Rees and his "prayer soldiers" had established a daily prayer routine, usually spending many hours each evening on their knees. When King George VI declared a day of prayer as troops gathered at Dunkirk in what many predicted to be a disastrous day for the British Expeditionary Force, Rees and his own "troops" prayed all the more fervently.

With some 338,000 Allied soldiers immobilized and penned in at Dunkirk, a horrific slaughter was feared. Under perilous circumstances, a mass evacuation from the French beaches began. Rees's biographer Norman Grubb tells us:

> On May 28 Mr. Howells again was alone with God. In the meetings, the prayer was for God to intervene at Dunkirk and save the men. As the Spirit came upon them in prayer and supplication, what one prayed at the end expressed the assurance given to all: "I feel sure something has happened."
>
> May 29 was the day of the evacuation of Dunkirk. Mr. Howells said, "Let us be clear in our prayer that the intercession is gained. The battle is the Holy Spirit's. See Him outside yourselves tonight; He is there on the battlefield with His drawn sword."[45]

Many years later, one of Howells's students, Ruth Williams—by then a well-coiffed, elegant elderly lady—recalled what it had been like that day. Once Howells had finished praying, he had opened the floor to others to pray, and she recalled that one man, "when he prayed, you knew that he had touched the Lord that time. It was amazing what happened in Dunkirk. The seas were so calm. . . . But God had His purpose, didn't He? He had said that Christian England wouldn't be invaded. And He was proving it to us."[46]

Though the fighting continued and many lives were lost, the successful evacuation of hundreds of thousands of soldiers later became known as "the Miracle of Dunkirk." It happened despite the best efforts of the UK government, which ran out of resources to help. Rather, hundreds of English civilians stepped into the gap, embarking in fishing boats and tugboats, anything to get soldiers and refugees back across the English Channel. And in Wales, a handful of students went to battle with the dark forces looming in Europe to turn the minds of those who would pursue and devour the retreating Allies.

Rees and those gathered at the school continued to pray for protection from invasion throughout the Battle of Britain up until the culminating day in September 1940 when the Luftwaffe, at the very moment of victory, turned and flew back to the mainland because Hitler had suddenly decided to invade Russia instead. As former British prime minister Winston Churchill recorded in a memoir about the war:

> I now asked: "What other reserves have we?" "There are none," said Air Vice-Marshal Park. In an account which he wrote about it afterwards, he said that at this I "looked grave." Well I might. . . .
>
> Another five minutes passed, and most of our squadrons had now descended to refuel. In many cases our resources could not give them overhead protection. Then it appeared that the enemy were going home. The shifting of the discs on the table

below showed a continuous eastward movement of German bombers and fighters. No new attack appeared. In another ten minutes the action was ended.[47]

At the very moment of strategic advantage and potential victory, Hitler "bent" in a different direction. He made another inconceivable decision that those unfamiliar with the power of prayer would scratch their heads over for decades: he turned on his Russian allies and invaded their lands, spurring them to join the Allies and eventually be among the victors of the war. It was an incredibly poor and arrogant decision, one so many dictators have made that it has become a saying: "Never invade Russia in winter." The Nazis found themselves in a quagmire, similar to Russian soldiers' finding themselves stranded and confounded by mud in the early days of the Ukraine War of 2022.

The Nazis turned south and east. When Italy couldn't defeat Greece, Germany invaded it and decided to take the island of Crete, believing that it was a key site from which to launch planes to protect their troops in North Africa. They thought they could take the island in days. But the battle dragged on, delaying the Nazi push to take Leningrad and Moscow into the winter, which eventually became a factor in their defeats there. Neither city ever fell to the Nazis, though they were again within hours of victory in each before other factors turned their attention. In his book *I Chose Freedom*, Victor Kravchenko wrote, "The Germans could have taken Moscow those days virtually without a struggle. . . . Why they turned back is a mystery only the Germans themselves can solve for history."[48]

Rees's college had continued to pray, battle by battle, day by day, for the Allied soldiers in all of those situations. "It's only with walking with God, isn't it?" said Ruth Williams when asked how one can become an intercessor as Howells and his students did. "I can't see that you can gain a position of intercession any other way but by walking daily with God and by praying daily and believing God."

Rees also had to learn how to live the Sermon on the Mount in the same way Maurice Reuben had. Once he found himself confronted by a man whose life had fallen apart because he was so deeply in debt.

As Rees saw him walk by the mission, he said, "I had never before known such a conflict for a soul in the spiritual realm. For an hour it was as much as I could do to allow the Holy Spirit to pray through me. I saw the devil attacking him. . . . I told the Lord I would do anything, if He would keep him."

Meeting the man later that day, Rees asked how far back the debt went. He said it was two years' worth of rent, squandered by his drinking habit. The man's creditors were seizing his furniture that very day.

"It was quite a huge sum in those days," said Rees's son, Samuel. His father's response was "I'll give you half, and I'm sure a friend of mine will give you the other half."

But as Rees walked up the stairs, going for the money, the Lord spoke to him, and he suddenly felt great shame. Rees said the Lord told him, "Didn't you tell Me this morning that you would give *all* you had to save him? Why are you only giving him half? Did not the Savior pay *all* your debt and set you free?" Rees swung around and ran back to the man, apologizing profusely and explaining that he would pay the man's rent in full, so that the man would no longer be vulnerable to the Devil. "The moment I said that the joy of heaven came down," Rees later said. "It was as if something snapped in my nature, and it became more blessed to give than to receive." Finally, he had come to live the Sermon on the Mount himself.

As Field Marshal Erwin Rommel's 90th Light Panzer Division closed in on the conquest of Egypt in July 1942, Rees felt that a line in the sand had to be drawn there. If the Nazis took Egypt, they could easily take Palestine, which Rees felt sure must be preserved for a Jewish homeland after the war. With the fighting at its fiercest, the students devoted themselves to praying that the Nazis would be stopped before taking Alexandria. The following week they learned in the papers that the Nazis had been defeated and surrendered at El Alamein. A primary factor in defeat: an almost total lack of fresh water, which had caused the German forces to become parched and dehydrated. More than a thousand surrendered due to extreme thirst.

As one editor commented in a magazine article, "Such an incredible happening as this cannot be treated as a mere coincidence. Assuredly the hand of Almighty God is in evidence once more, coming to our aid when weighty issues are in the balance."[49]

The students at the Welsh college continued to pray throughout the remainder of the war, and in battle after battle the Nazis were turned back until Allied troops marched into Berlin in final victory in Europe on May 8, 1945.

After the war ended, the college poured missionaries into the field and also continued to pray. It was a great blessing of his life that Rees and his students, who had stood with the Jews all the years of the war, were part of praying for and then witnessing a Jewish homeland being founded in Palestine on May 14, 1948. (Notably, the man whose faith had inspired Rees to become a Christian, Maurice Reuben, was Jewish.) Rees called the event:

One of the greatest days for the Holy Spirit in the history of these two thousand years. . . .

During all those centuries there wasn't a single sign that the country was to be given back to the Jews who were scattered all over the earth; but now, four thousand years after His covenant with Abraham, He has gathered all the nations together and made them give much of the land of Palestine back to them.[50]

For the rest of his life, Rees continued to pray that the Gospel would go out to every person without hindrance. After a final prayer request to provide £100,000 for the future of the Bible school "was won," Rees went on to meet his Maker face-to-face. He passed away on February 13, 1950, and his last words were, "Victory . . . Hallelujah!"

HE NEEDED A MIRACLE

In a moment of crisis, Gary found himself turning to the
story of a man in the Bible who had lost everything.

> Let us then approach God's throne of grace with
> confidence, so that we may receive mercy and find
> grace to help us in our time of need.
>
> —HEBREWS 4:16

Job's biggest question was *why*. He'd been a success his whole
life. He had ten children, and the hills of his land were covered with his livestock. He was the big man in town. Whenever
Job walked into the city, young men stepped aside out of respect.
He was respected—and good. He was "a father to the poor." He
was "eyes to the blind . . . feet to the lame."

Job did everything right. So why did he lose everything?

Lying in a hospital bed with a 1.7 percent chance to live in early
2020, Gary couldn't stop thinking about the Book of Job. What

had started as a routine bout with the flu had descended into sepsis, placing Gary's life in danger.

Gary's crisis had come as suddenly as Job's. A healthy athlete his entire life, Gary had found it a shock when body aches, chills, a head-to-toe rash, and shortness of breath had sent him to the ER four times in five days just after Christmas 2019. "I had chest pain like a heart attack," he said. "I felt like there was glass in my throat. My resting heart rate was 110."

By New Year's Eve, Gary was in full-blown septic shock, his organs were shutting down, and his friends and family were urged to hurry to his hospital bedside in Rockledge, Florida, to say their final goodbyes.

It was a stunning turn of events for Gary, who just days before had been living the all-American dad life. Like Job, he had "won" at life. At thirty-eight years old, he found the work-life balance that many thirtysomethings save for "someday." He had traded in seventy-hour workweeks as a car salesman for a home-based digital marketing sales job that allowed him to be present with his four kids, then ages five, seven, eight, and fifteen. The payoff had been sanity, a robust retirement account, and the opportunity for Gary, a two-time Florida track champion, to coach his kids' sports teams.

Gary's days moved at a predictable suburban cadence: he loaded the kids into his SUV every morning and took them to school, worked a nine-to-five job, coached his kids' sports teams on evenings and Saturdays, and attended church on Sundays.

In 2019, Gary and his family had a wonderful Christmas. No one knew it was going to be the last normal day for a long time.

One week later, on January 1, 2020, Gary was airlifted to a hospital in Orlando that had an extracorporeal membrane oxygenation, or ECMO, machine, a device similar to a heart-lung bypass machine used to keep patients alive during open-heart surgery. He didn't fully understand the swirl of monitors, probes, medications, and decisions that was overtaking his life. He remembered a doctor telling his family not to get their hopes up. Then he flatlined.

Gary's last name, by the way, was Miracle. Unconscious and teetering near death for more than eleven minutes, the man who'd been teased mercilessly as a kid about his name—"Miracle Whip, MiracleGro, I heard them all," he said—now needed an actual miracle. The first one happened immediately, as the doctor on call happened to be a cardiologist, the first of many dominoes that needed to fall correctly in order for Gary to survive. The doctor resuscitated him and whisked him into a five-hour surgery to connect him to the ECMO machine.

Gary doesn't remember what came next. He had slipped into a coma and was dependent on the machine to recirculate oxygen-rich blood to his core organs. He descended into a terrifying internal journey in which vivid, prolonged nightmares tormented him with the same theme: "I was always trapped somewhere, able to see life go on outside but screaming and pounding on glass to try to get someone to notice me and let me out," Gary said.

Days passed. Unseen by Gary, in his hospital room, a vibrant world of prayer and faith encircled him. Friends and family held his hands, stroked his hair, and never left him alone for a second. They prayed that his 1.7 percent chance of survival was enough for God to work with. They pleaded with God to let Gary live.

On Christmas in 2019, Gary's family had posed for the quintessential family picture in the lobby of their church. At the time, the photo had seemed unremarkable. Gary later realized that it was the last photo he had where he was clasping his children's shoulders with his own hands.

After ten days of coma nightmares, Gary woke to see the walls of his hospital room covered with scriptures and family photos. "My family wanted to make sure the doctors and nurses knew who they were saving—a dad, husband, brother, son, and friend," he said.

Then he looked down. His hands and legs were black. The cost of saving his heart, kidneys, lungs, and brain had been paid by his extremities. His hands and legs were discolored and cold, casualties of an irreversible disease process caused by lack of blood and oxygen. Called necrosis, the term was explained to Gary with words such as *decay*, *death*, and a terrifying process that seemed as though it was closing in on all of him: *mummification*.

Two weeks later, Gary's dad decided it was time for a father-son talk, the kind no dad ever wants to have with his son. He asked everyone to leave the hospital room and explained that the legs that had once won races would have to be amputated. The hands that had closed a thousand deals with a firm shake? Gary would lose those, too.

"I think it was almost too hard to believe," Gary said. Living in the fog of a cocktail of twenty-seven daily medications, he now had to process the idea of life as a quadruple amputee. It was a key moment. How would he respond?

Gary said that learning he'd live limbless provided a glimpse into his indomitable faith. He told his dad, "The Lord gives, and the Lord takes away. Right now, it's time for him to take away my arms and legs, but I will say, 'Blessed be the name of the Lord.'"

Gary insists that he's not some super-Christian, Sunday-school-answer type of guy. But ever since age ten, when he had decided to follow the Lord, a cornerstone belief in his life has been that *God is good*. Before entering sales, he had served as a youth pastor, a calling he'd explored after running merchandise sales for an up-and-coming band, MercyMe.

"I had spent my life telling people and preaching that God was good," he explained. "Now that something traumatic happened in my life, was I going to live like God *wasn't* good?"

His family's faith helped boost Gary's spirits. His family and friends came frequently to pray. Gary recalled several occasions when he had looked at machines registering bleak vital signs, only to have friends gather around him, anoint him with oil, and pray for healing. "I'd look up, and the numbers would be instantly different," he said.

Once amputation had become inevitable, Gary's family prayed that he would lose his limbs below the elbow and knee joints, rather than above them. It wasn't a given, as Gary's tissues were badly damaged. Yet keeping those joints would allow him greater dexterity with prosthetics.

On March 17, Gary lost his hands. Eight days later, doctors amputated his left leg. On April 22, he lost his right leg. But he kept both elbows and both knees.

As Gary's time in the hospital dragged on, he followed Job's arc exactly, growing isolated from a world where he had once been central. Confined to a hospital room for months, with access only to a streaming movie service, he had no idea that COVID-19 was sweeping the globe. When his health care team began caring for him wearing head-to-toe personal protective equipment, he thought he was somehow putting *them* at risk. "I thought it was me," he recalled. He didn't understand that the face shields, gowns, and gloves were designed to protect *him* from the virus, which could have dealt a fatal blow to his fragile immune system.

Finally, it was time to go home. Having been airlifted to the hospital on New Year's Day weighing 240 pounds, Gary left on April Fool's Day weighing 155 pounds, a cruel indicator of both his reduced body mass and the limbs he had lost.

Transitioning from hospital to home meant that Gary's recovery also transitioned—from harrowing to grueling. One wasn't any easier than the other. Hallways, once wide enough for a hands-on dad to race through them in spirited games of tag, were now narrow and restrictive for a limbless man tasked with maneuvering a motorized wheelchair.

For Gary, simply holding a travel mug meant cradling it at just the right angle against his chest and inside his elbow joints, all to win the victory of a possible sip. More often than not, he dropped the mug, just as he dropped his phone, shampoo bottle, and many other objects he had previously held on to without a thought.

It was a hard lesson in humility. The old Gary had mastered the art of closing the deal, looked the Christian part in church, been all things to all people, and always "had it together." Now there was no more pretending. Things he'd done in seconds before, such as flinging dirty laundry into the washing machine or using eating utensils, seemed like tasks too fine tuned for a man with blunt limbs.

"There was a line in the sand for me when I got home," he said. "I could sit on the couch, live a pity party, get addicted to pain pills, and live that life. Or I could pick one thing a day to master." He chose the latter, devoting himself first to learning how to plug his cell phone into its charger, daring the phone's battery not to die before his strength did. "It took three hours for me to do it that first time," he recalled.

Through sweat, tears, and occasionally burying his face into his pillow to muffle his guttural cries, he relearned how to load the washing machine with dirty clothes. He mastered the art of getting dressed by himself, and he mustered the dignity of using the restroom alone.

For as many tasks as he relearned, there were also abilities he learned for the first time—hard things for an athletic, self-sufficient man to admit he needed, such as being vulnerable and asking for help. One day he sat too low on the sofa to hoist himself into his wheelchair and slid unceremoniously into a heap on the floor, where he remained until help arrived. Another day, he pulled too hard on the toilet paper roll, ripping the dispenser off the wall. The dismantled fixture clanked to the ground, an unintended metaphor for his own amputation and loss of function. Rather than get depressed, he asked a friend to reinstall the toilet paper roll.

But out of so much loss, something new was growing. The church, his family, and his friends literally became Gary's hands and feet. They helped with everything the Miracles needed: meals, household cleaning, yardwork, and most especially prayer. Soon enough, Gary would be able to join them, clasping his own "hands" in prayer, too.

In summer 2020, he received long-awaited, custom prosthetic arms and hands. Not only did the black pinchers elicit *oohs* and *ahhhs* from his kids, but they reintroduced dexterity for Gary. Then, in 2021, he received three sets of custom prosthetic legs, including a slick pair of running blades that he used to participate in a local two-mile fun run just one month later and a pair of water blades that enabled him to swim at the beach.

To keep his biceps strong, Gary cradled a dumbbell bar in his elbows and lifted it tightly to his chest. To keep up his sense of humor, he posted social media messages, such as a photo of him sitting on the floor with his prosthetic limbs next to him. The caption read, "I'm beside myself."

He consistently read the scriptures, pressing hard into the Bible's account of Job. "There's a verse, Job 42:5, that basically says: 'All my life I've heard about you with my ears, but for the first time I've seen you with my eyes,'" he said.

The verse made sense to Gary, who now saw a clear path into ministry. Even as a youth minister, his call into ministry had not mobilized him to tell others about his faith in Jesus like recovery from trauma did. Through his ministry, Gary Miracle Speaks, he began traveling all over the United States, encouraging audiences to bring their struggles and failures into full view. "The only difference between me and other people is my struggles are visible," he explained. "Sometimes invisible struggles are even scarier. I beg people to risk it, to find one person they can share their struggles with."

Featured prominently in the video for the hit song "Say I Won't," written for him by his friends in MercyMe, Gary watched his ministry explode with speaking engagements, podcast bookings, and expanded social media presence. He began an autobiography, launched a website, and even developed a merchandise line incorporating his own EKG reading into his logo. The reading shows his first pulse after eleven minutes of flatlining in 2020.

The new life God has given Gary is a lot to take in. Limb by limb, he lost his body, but God gave him greater reach. And the man who once won races learned to run the race God set before him. Even if it meant running without his own legs.

It's easy to look at Gary's story and fixate on his recovery. But just as remarkable was the moment when he chose to trust God. "The Lord gives and the Lord takes away" is a sentence that's both heartbreaking and comforting. It is an acknowledgment of

God's power over everything in our life. Gary's decision to *still* say, "Blessed be the name of the Lord" is a reminder that it's possible, in the depths of darkness, to praise God. In fact, remembering the goodness of God is vital to weathering life's darkest times.

That line is a quote from Job. Sitting in the dust, having lost his children, his riches, and finally his health within the space of days, Job felt abandoned. But still Job said, "The Lord gave, and the Lord has taken away. Blessed be the name of the Lord."

What makes that possible? We have to remember that God promises to come alongside us in our troubles. Job laments that God "is not a mere mortal like me, that I might answer Him, that we might confront each other to court. If only there were someone to mediate between us, someone to bring us together." (Job 9:32–33)

Gary Miracle has a big advantage over Job. Living many centuries before Christ, Job could only dream of a "mediator," of someone who could step into his life and suffer alongside him. Gary knows the reality that God really did step into this world, take on flesh, and suffer alongside us. Pain, humiliation, vulnerability, powerlessness—Jesus willingly took on our human weaknesses and still remains our mediator with His father.

"I can do all things/Through Christ who gives me strength," go the lyrics of MercyMe's song "Say I Won't," quoting Scripture. But the next line transitions to Gary's mantra: "So keep on saying I won't/And I'll keep proving you wrong."

It's okay to grieve when we suffer tragedies. What the stories of Job and Gary Miracle underline is that that's the time when we must draw close to God. In our weakness is His strength.

A FIREFIGHTER'S DREAM

A woman shows us how to keep your faith until you
experience supernatural peace after tragedy.

> The peace of God, which transcends all
> understanding, will guard your hearts and your
> minds in Christ Jesus.
>
> —PHILIPPIANS 4:7

Sixteen-year-old Ann Clark gazed around the theater. She imagined it packed to the seams with avid fans. Their cheers and smiles lifted her spirits right up to the gilded cream-and-orange ceiling. She couldn't believe it. She was on a real Broadway stage—holy ground for a theater kid from New Jersey.

Then the music started. Ann tumbled back to earth. It was her first audition, and there were only four people in the audience. She was surrounded by other dancers, all of them just as determined as she was to make the grade. Caught up in her dream, she'd lost track of what she was doing. In an instant she readjusted and began moving in tandem with the girls to her right and left, careful to keep her balance on the raked stage.

She smiles at the memory now. "The thing about ballet," she said, "is you never really hit perfection."

Unlike team sports, ballet is highly individual. There's always someone who is better. There's always something about your own performance that isn't perfect, some fault that must be corrected, no reality that is as perfect as a dream.

After the audition ended, walking to the bus stop, Ann found herself so captivated by the experience of being onstage that she barely cared about the role itself. That glow didn't dissipate on the bus ride home or when she walked into the house with a huge grin on her face. When Ann's mom saw her daughter's expression, she grabbed her husband's arm. "Oh, my God! She got the part!"

But Ann shook her head, beaming. "No. But I stood on a real Broadway stage." She had found a different dream. Even though she hadn't gotten the part, the magical emotion she'd felt onstage had lit a fire for her true passion: sharing that feeling with the world.

Ann was born in Oxford, England, to a British mother and an American father. The family moved to the United States when Ann was two, eventually settling in New Jersey, across the Hudson River from New York City.

By sixteen, Ann had fallen in love with dance and spent her afternoons teaching at a dance studio and auditioning for Broadway musicals. Teaching enabled her to share her joy with others in a special way. She truly felt that it was her calling. When, at twenty-one, she lost her job as a dance instructor, she was devastated. She came home in a deep gloom and collapsed into a chair next to her dad. Out flooded a stream of emotional complaints.

After letting the complaints subsided, Ann's dad redirected her. "Okay," he said calmly. "What are you going do now? What do you want to do?"

Gathering herself, Ann pondered, then the answer came to her: "I want to teach little girls ballet."

"And what do you need to do that?" her dad asked.

"Well, I need space," Ann replied. "Maybe ballet barres. And I guess a record player."

"That's a good start," he said. "You'll also need a name for your business, and you're going to need a bank account."

They sat down at the dining room table and made a list.

Ann didn't know it, but her life was being lived in parallel with another young person, thinking wistfully of a dream. A lanky veteran, Bruce Van Hine had spent his youth in the navy. Later, he became an arborist. But he'd always had a secret, unlikely dream: he wanted to be a firefighter.

In 1973, he read *Report from Engine Co. 82*, a book chronicling the life of a firefighting crew in the South Bronx. "Those people in the book seemed out of reach," he later wrote.

Raised in a Christian family, Bruce found faith an essential pillar of his life. He spent a lot of his time hiking. Traveling the Appalachian Trail in the northeast, he would leave Bibles at every shelter.

For Ann, faith didn't come so easily. "I learned a lot about the Bible and all that growing up, and I understood all that. But the idea of a relationship . . . you could have a relationship with Jesus?"

She'd been attending a Bible study and she was intrigued by what they said about Christ. Sensing she needed to know more, she went to a Christian bookstore. "I was, like, looking around at stuff. And I think they asked, 'Can we help you?'" she said. After she explained what was going on in her life, "the guy just asked me if I wanted to accept Jesus as my savior."

She said yes. It changed everything. She'd always thought of God as something distant, just someone "in charge," far away. But now He was present in her life every day.

One of her favorite biblical stories describes God speaking to Moses through a burning bush. (Exodus 3:4–12) In the story, God explained that He wouldn't just help Moses, He would be close to him.

Moses faced the same problem that Ann did: a dream that didn't manifest itself. Born a Hebrew slave, Moses became an adopted prince in the kingdom of Egypt, thousands of years before Christ. Moses thought he knew which way his life was going. He'd been put into the Egyptian palace for a reason, surely. He had a plan: he was going to use his privilege as a prince to overthrow cruel rulers and defend slaves. That dream, noble as it was, got crushed pretty quickly; he was exiled after killing an abusive slave overseer.

The way it came about stung: the man he had defended, rather than keeping Moses' secret, instead spread the news as vicious gossip. On the run for murder, Moses fled Egypt and found shelter among a nomadic tribe in the land of Midian. He spent the next forty years of his life tending sheep in the desert. (Exodus 2:11–45)

It was during one of those interminable years that Moses saw a bush, crackling with fire—but for some reason, though the bush was alight, it didn't disintegrate in the flames. Out of the fire, God spoke to Moses. He asked Moses to do something really hard. "I have indeed seen the misery of my people in Egypt," He told Moses. "I have heard them crying out because of their slave drivers, and I am concerned about their suffering. . . . So now, go. I am sending you to Pharaoh to bring my people the Israelites out of Egypt."

"Who am I," Moses asked, "that I should go to Pharaoh and bring the Israelites out of Egypt?"

God said, "I will be with you."

Through the journey of starting her own ballet school (which was a big deal for a twenty-one-year-old woman, especially in 1975), Ann sometimes thought to herself, *I'm barely an adult, and this is going to be hard work! Who am I to start a business?* But her dad was there with her every step of the way. God was, too.

And increasingly, so was Bruce Van Hine. The day Ann lost her job was also the day she met Bruce. He literally showed up on her doorstep, the friend of a friend who dropped in for a visit. It wasn't quite love at first sight. After their first date, Ann told a friend she thought he was a creep.

Ann and Bruce married in 1980, and after the embarrassment wore off, she often affectionately joked that he was "my creep." Though the world of theater and dance was foreign to him, he was a tireless cheerleader for Ann's efforts. He'd always take the day off when Ann's annual recital took place, so he could help set up and cheer her on.

Bruce owned a tree service business, but it was seasonal work and he spent the off-season looking for odd jobs. It didn't make budgeting easy for the young family. One morning, as he scanned the newspaper for work, Ann sat down with him at the kitchen table. She studied her husband for a few moments as he circled want ads. She thought of all she'd learned over the years, the way her dreams had changed, but she'd always chased them. "What did you always want to be when you grew up?" she asked.

He didn't hesitate for a moment. "A firefighter." He paused, then emphasized, "A *real* firefighter."

"Real?"

"A New York City firefighter," he said.

"Then do that."

Bruce applied for training in 1981. He would finally be accepted at the Fire Department of the City of New York (FDNY) in 1990, his application having gotten caught up in red tape. In the meantime, he worked as a firefighter at West Point. For many years, he didn't think his dream—to become a "real" firefighter—would happen. His application remained lodged firmly in red tape.

But finally he achieved his dream. He became a member of the FDNY.

It was a moment that brought him tremendous pride. He wrote to his wife, "I never thought I had what it took to be a firefighter in the Big Apple. This could not have been possible without your encouragement and love. I thank the Lord for you and this day. I'll always love you."[51]

"ALL FIREFIGHTERS REPORT FOR DUTY."

It was eleven years later. Ann Van Hine took her eyes off the highway long enough to reach over and turn up the volume on the car radio. She knew that New York didn't call firefighters into work over the radio. Something very unusual must be happening.

"Is this an act of terrorism?" the newscaster asked. "Is the country at war?"

It was the morning of September 11, 2001, and no one knew anything for sure. The only certain thing was that two planes had crashed into the twin towers of the World Trade Center.

Lord, please protect Bruce, Ann prayed. *Bring him home.*

Ann picked up their two teenage daughters early from school. Since the phone networks were overwhelmed, Ann drove straight to her parents' house. "Sweetheart, I'm sure Bruce is safe," her father said, seeking to calm her nerves. "From the time they called for everyone to report to duty, Bruce wouldn't have had time to get from his station house in the Bronx all the way to Lower Manhattan before the towers fell."

Ann wasn't convinced. Impressively, when Bruce had finally been hired at FDNY, he had immediately gone out with a truck (a unique feat, a former colleague of his explained in a US Army website interview in 2020). He had then become part of Squad 41, a Special Operations Command unit. Ann knew that firefighters in squads did things on a daily basis that other units couldn't or wouldn't—dangerous things they didn't tell their spouses about. Being part of that squad, Bruce and his colleagues would have been dispatched to the towers sooner rather than later.

Shortly before midnight, Ann heard a car outside. She fought the temptation to look out the window. Please don't be coming here, she prayed. She answered the knock at the door to find two firemen. She ushered the pair inside, where the three of them stood awkwardly in silence.

"Just say it," Ann finally said.

"He is unaccounted for."

IN THE FOLLOWING DAYS, ANN could barely think, much less concentrate. Processing anything new felt overwhelming, so she returned over and over to familiar passages of Scripture she'd read countless times before.

She often read Philippians 4:8: "Finally, brothers and sisters, whatever is true, whatever is noble, whatever is right, whatever is pure, whatever is lovely, whatever is admirable—if anything is excellent or praiseworthy—think about such things."

One day her eyes scanned up the page to the preceding passage, to words that felt as though they had been written just for that moment, just for her:

> Rejoice in the Lord always. I will say it again: Rejoice! Let your gentleness be evident to all. The Lord is near. Do not be anxious about anything, but in every situation, by prayer and petition, with thanksgiving, present your requests to God. And the peace of God, which transcends all understanding, will guard your hearts and your minds in Christ Jesus.
>
> —PHILIPPIANS 4:4–7

Ann experienced that peace often when she prayed. But that day something else about the verse grabbed her attention: "The Lord is near."

She remembered her favorite story in the Bible: the burning bush. "Who am I," Moses had asked, "that I should go to Pharaoh and bring the Israelites out of Egypt?"

And God had said, "I will be with you."

It struck Ann that God hadn't really answered Moses' question. He hadn't explained why he had chosen Moses for that task even if Moses felt inadequate. He hadn't pulled the "God card" and said, "Don't ask questions, just do what I'm telling you to do." He hadn't even told Moses why it was important for him to do that difficult thing. His answer had been far more personal and powerful. He'd simply said, "I'll be with you."

When Ann had started her business at twenty-one, it had been challenging, but her dad had walked with her the whole way.

Now she was facing something that was excruciatingly difficult, harder than anything else she had ever done: going into the unknown without Bruce at her side.

And her heavenly Father was saying, "I'll be with you."

ON TUESDAY, SEPTEMBER 18, ONE week after the towers fell, Ann attended an FDNY meeting in the city. There, in a vast hotel ballroom in the heart of Manhattan, the mayor, the governor, the FDNY commissioner, and the medical examiner told an audience of spouses and family members what many of them already suspected.

"No one's been found alive for the last five days," an official announced. "It's time to change the focus from rescue to recovery." He looked down. "It's time to bring in the heavy machinery."

The other firefighters weren't ready to give up. They kept searching, kept digging, kept hoping.

But Ann knew Bruce wasn't coming home. The family didn't have his body. The recovery workers would probably never find it.

When she started planning a memorial service for Bruce, the girls had questions. "What if we're wrong?" they asked. "What if they find Daddy?"

"I would like nothing more than for Daddy to walk into his own service," Ann said gently.

The memorial service took place on September 29, 2001. Ann and her family arrived at the church to find a huge American flag suspended between two FDNY ladder trucks. The service was filled with singing and prayer, memories and tears. Somehow they made it through. When at last it was time to leave the church, Ann and the girls walked past a formation of firefighters standing outside.

There was no skirling sound of bagpipes; Ann had decided that she simply couldn't bear that. It would have been too much. Instead, all she can remember is the utter silence as the firefighters stared straight ahead. The only sound was the click of her shoes on the sidewalk.

ANN'S MOTHER HAD GROWN UP in England during World War II, while bombs were falling, and had always said, "Americans don't know what it is like to have your homeland attacked."

Now they knew.

After September 11, families like Ann's found themselves grieving very personal losses in a highly charged, public arena. The bombings had shocked the nation and the world—and everyone wanted to support and honor the families of the fallen.

Ann and her daughters were invited to hundreds of special events. They met celebrities and received countless gifts, including the first new car Ann had ever owned.

Ann resumed teaching at the dance studio. There she was still "Miss Ann," but everywhere else she was now "Mrs. Van Hine, FDNY widow." She gave a few interviews to the media following 9/11, and on several occasions, she was asked to "say a few words" at some event or other.

In 2005, the family was invited to a White House ceremony where Ann was presented with a Congressional Medal of Valor on Bruce's behalf. In 2016, she was invited to speak to the European Parliament.

She remembers talking to God about that one: "Lord, what are they thinking? Who am I to go talk to the European Parliament?"

And as she heard her own words, she remembered Moses's question to God. Most important, she remembered what God had told Moses—and what he'd been telling her on every step of this journey: "I'll be with you."

By March 2006, Ann was leading walking tours around the construction site where the World Trade Center had once stood. She calls herself "a keeper of stories" and says God has used volunteering with the 9/11 Tribute Museum to speak to her in many ways. To date, she has led more than five hundred such tours, and in that time she has seen the completion of the 9/11 Memorial Plaza, the 9/11 Memorial Museum, and finally Liberty Park, as well as the rise of the Freedom Tower.

She wrote a memoir about her journey titled *Pieces Falling: Navigating 9/11 with Faith, Family, and the FDNY.* She continues to volunteer with the 9/11 Tribute Museum.

"Sometimes dreams morph and change," she said. "My dream of dancing on Broadway morphed into a beloved career of teaching little girls how to dance. Bruce's abandoned dream of being a New York firefighter was rediscovered and reborn. My dream—growing old with the man I loved—died on 9/11, and I've had to embrace new dreams. But whatever life brings, I know God can be trusted. Even when I don't like or don't understand what is happening, I know I'm not alone. I know He's walking that journey with me."

A PRAYER IN EL SANTUARIO DE CHIMAYÓ

Pilgrimages remind us of the importance of seeking a God
who speaks back.

> You will seek me and find me when you seek me
> with all your heart.
>
> —JEREMIAH 29:13

Seven-year-old Austin Canon ran his hand along the fraying seat of his father's Oldsmobile. The air was musty from the powerful dry heat of a Texas summer. But his dad was driving and they were together. It was going to be a good day.

Austin's dad wasn't talkative by nature. Rather than shyness, though, a quiet strength radiated off the man. His son would later learn he had gained this stoicism enduring the horrors of Iwo Jima. He never talked about what he'd been through there.

That day seemed like any other, but Austin and his dad were about to be miracle workers for a stranger.

Idly staring ahead of them, Austin gasped when he saw a truck roll violently off the highway. He yelled, pointing ahead. His dad was already moving smoothly into action, pulling their car off the road.

Austin remembers how calm his dad was, striding purposefully toward the flipped car. Smoke and steam escaped from the engine compartment. The ex-Marine remained calm and grabbed the driver and swiftly and efficiently dragged him well clear of the wreck.

His father performed a quick examination of the man. His expression said it all: The man needed help as soon as possible.

Then he looked toward the overturned truck, assessing any possible further danger.

"You stay away from that truck, it's liable to catch fire," he told his son, who'd been edging closer to the wrecked vehicle in fascination.

The stranger was bloodied and unable to move himself. Austin's dad said to his son, "Keep with him, talk to him, and whatever you do, don't leave him."

Austin felt a surge of panic as he watched his father drive away to get help. What was he supposed to say or do? As he watched his father's car disappear into the distance he felt a mix of pride and fear. If his dad believed he could handle this, Austin thought, then he knew he could.

Austin knelt beside the man and spoke about the first thing he could think of that a farmer might know about—watermelons—how big they could grow and how much he liked eating them. The man nodded and muttered some form of a reply. Later a white-haired Austin would reflect on this and other incidents from his life, "When you're young you aren't as cognizant of the significance of the things that are happening around you. Great things could happen around you and be just 'things that happen.' In hindsight, you go, 'Wow, that was really quite amazing.'"

Now, Austin realizes the immense significance of their intervention for the injured driver. It probably saved his life. "For that man," he said, "us being right there was a miracle. In hindsight, that was the day I started to become a man."

Even though, to Austin, he and his father were just going down a normal, everyday road, they were really on a spiritual mission. Remembering that we're always alongside an invisible spiritual world fraught with risks and opportunities is vital to living the Christian life. That road we walk is often dark and winding. Trusting in God as we walk through difficult roads is something we all must do. We all have battles we must fight. The question, then, is what principles and practices help us walk through those valleys.

"When I was young, I was raised to be very independent, you know, free thinking," Austin said. Austin's father was with him throughout his childhood. King David wrote in a famous Psalm, "Yea, though I walk through the valley of the shadow of death, I will fear no evil: for thou art with me; thy rod and thy staff they comfort me." (Psalm 23:4, KJV)

David was talking of the way our heavenly Father is with us in the valleys of life. But Austin feels like his father has played a similar role in his life. Austin's dad, US Marine Corporal Robert Travis Canon, served his country with great distinction in World War II's Pacific Theater. He was among the 2nd wave that landed on Iwo Jima and served with the Marines 28th regiment, the unit that eventually raised the flag on that island.

"My dad saw a lot of horrible things in the war," Austin said. "He fought for six and half days on Iwo Jima before he was wounded and evacuated onto a hospital ship." Any soldier who survives combat has received the gift of a miracle. Corporal Canon saw, according to Austin, that "faith wasn't gonna protect him from a bullet. But his faith was going to keep him strong, and working, and forward-thinking, and helping his fellow man. Faith was going to make his world easier to deal with. And it did. He survived the war."

Austin, obviously, is a product of that faith. But when he wanted to follow the same path, his father had an unexpected response. "My dad smiled. He kind of laughed and said, 'Don't join. Go to college.' Then he said to my brother and me, 'I've done enough time for both of you.'"

That spirit of service still informed Austin's life. So did his father's attitude. He would remind his boys frequently that any bad day they were facing, any tough circumstances they encountered could be overcome. They had to keep a positive attitude. After all, anything they faced wasn't as bad as a day in combat.

The day of the car wreck, Austin knew that for his father, faith meant believing that car wouldn't blow up as he approached it. "He was doing the right thing by helping that man and by doing the right thing, in turn, he believed he'd be taken care of," Austin explained.

God never truly leaves us alone, but it is true that He can send us on missions that feel too big for us. That's because He knows that we can't grow until we face those challenges. We shouldn't view life like a game. Suffering can be overwhelming and seem at the time like it's meaningless. But Paul reminds us that "suffering produces perseverance; perseverance, character; and character, hope. And hope does not put us to shame, because God's love has been poured out into our hearts through the Holy Spirit, who has been given to us." (Romans 5:3–5)

Austin has faced challenges throughout his life, but he believes that the strength instilled in him by his father has allowed him to endure. While he was raised a Christian, and has never truly lost that faith, he does feel that for years, his faith in God was pushed onto the backburner.

Austin had become distracted from faith over time. He's not alone in that. As our society has grown less religious, it has also grown less likely to believe God has the power to intervene at all when life is hard. Whereas 81 percent of Americans believe in God, according to a June 2022 Gallup Poll, half of those theistic Americans believe only in a powerless, distant God who doesn't answer prayers.

That's remarkable. It reminds us that it really isn't enough just to believe in God without qualifications. If you believe in God but don't believe that He acts, you're not only cutting yourself off from an incredible divine bounty but also choosing to pretend that nothing you do could ever get a reaction out of Him. It's like pretending you have a dad who doesn't care.

Austin received a powerful wakeup call on the morning of December 16, 2018. Normally he would get up on a Saturday morning, take a bike ride, take a long hike in the mountains, ski. But for some reason, that morning he decided to hang around a little bit and talk to a friend.

Austin now sees this as a first part of the miracle that changed his life. For a long time, Austin had just been coasting in his belief in an active God. But what happened that morning shook him out of his apathy. While sitting with his partner Laura Post, he experienced the first symptoms of a stroke. Laura was a long-time nurse and knew exactly what to do. Through her swift action, Austin was rushed to the emergency room and was seen immediately by medical personnel. Time was of the essence, and at each stage of the process, caring professionals were there for him. Later, Austin couldn't help but marvel at the fact that, had he taken that bike ride into the lightly traveled roads beyond the outskirts of town, the outcome might have been very different.

He believes that his attitude significantly helped him come through the experience. He remembered being by his father's death-bed and telling him jokes, reminding him of the good times. Now, Austin was doing for himself what he'd done for his father. "You can be serious as heck about everything. But you can also be light-hearted. You can still take on tough circumstances with courage."

When the nurse came in, she gave Austin a quizzical look. He was smiling. That was because he'd decided it was going to be a good day.

The hemorrhage didn't worsen. It lessened over the three days he was in critical care. Equally important, the hemorrhage occurred near Austin's brain stem, affecting motor function but not cognitive function. He didn't lose any of his memory or other critical mental functions. He did lose the ability to speak. He was paralyzed on the right side. He had to go through months of rehabilitative therapy in order to restore those functions. Now, he has a slight slur to his speech and some reduced dexterity, but his Texan-accented voice is clear and he's gotten back to some biking and skiing.

He found himself in a doctor's visit where she simply shook her head and said, "I have never seen a recovery like yours. Your outcome is a great exception to the rules of what happens when people have brain hemorrhages."

Austin came through the ordeal with a refreshed sense of God's faithfulness and presence. He attributes his healing to faith and positive thinking, but also, he said, "I really do believe in miracles."

Austin had heard of a place where believers go when they need a boost or a reconnection with the Lord.

It's beginning to get a lot more publicity these days as more and more people flock there. Maybe that's a recognition of today's circumstances. There is apparently a need to reach out and touch faith. Thousands of Americans make a pilgrimage to a tiny Chapel in New Mexico every year. The docent who is responsible for preserving the Chapel and its history shared with me that El Santuario de Chimayó is a place where people can walk in the footsteps of Jesus. It's literally a faith walk! Curiosity draws people to take the dusty, meaningful walk through the New Mexico heat.

After Austin had recovered enough from his stroke, he decided out of gratitude to undertake a pilgrimage to a small holy place in the desert, where he would remember the sacrifice of a different man, not a stranger, but our greatest friend.

He describes it this way: the walk feels like a culmination to many events in his life. A journey, a spiritual mission, memory, fatherhood, a deep desire to help others.

Before the stroke, this eight-mile walk would have presented few challenges for Austin. Over the years he had grown to be an avid outdoorsman and adventurer who loved skiing and mountaineering. But despite his remarkable recovery, the hike would push him.

"I've been to El Santuario de Chimayó quite a few times, but I've never taken the walk," Austin recalled. He joined a group from Santa Fe, New Mexico's Church of the Holy Faith. The group would drive to Nambé Pueblo, the home of a federally recognized tribe of Native American people. From there, they would begin an eight-mile hike that would take them to El Santuario de Chimayó.

In so doing, they would be participating in a Holy Week pilgrimage which originates in the Via Dolorosa in Jerusalem. This is no mere "hike." Instead, it is a journey commemorating what Jesus endured on Good Friday leading to his crucifixion and death. All around the world, in churches, through the streets of towns large and small, this Good Friday service is known as the Stations of the Cross. The fourteen stations—each representing an event in Jesus' journey—begin with Jesus being condemned to death and end with His body being placed in a tomb. At each station, the participants stop and pray, reflecting on the Passion of Christ and His suffering prior to his triumphant resurrection.

The Stations of the Cross at El Santuario de Chimayó are a physical re-enactment of what Christ endured. Some pilgrims carry a wooden cross; others approach on their knees. We can read the accounts of those hours in the Bible. We can see films depicting it, but sometimes we both desire and need to walk the walk ourselves to fully understand and appreciate our Lord and Savior's sacrifice. God understands our human weakness. Whether resembling Jesus' disciple Thomas, saying, "Unless I see the nail marks in his hands and put my finger where the nails were, and put my hands into his side, I will not believe" (John 20:25) or the myriad other ways in which we question and doubt, we often fall short of being among those "who have not seen and yet have believed." (John 20:29)

A valuable insight which the Stations of the Cross emphasizes is that we are embodied creatures who need physical reinforcement of what we know mentally. In His infinite wisdom and grace, God has instructed us to perform physical rituals in addition to the intellectual exercises of reading Scripture and praying.

Patricia Trujillo-Oviedo is a tour guide and historian at El Santuario de Chimayó. Thousands of individuals make a pilgrimage each year. She estimates that thirty thousand of them come during the Holy Week walk. Many are drawn to the small adobe church seeking mental, physical, and spiritual healing attributed to the "holy dirt" that was left over when, long before the Spanish came to the area, a hot spring existed and then dried up. El Santuario De Chimayó is often compared to Lourdes, France, another site of miraculous healings.

Two chapels stand on the site. One, the Holy Child of Atocha Chapel, was erected by Severiano Medina in gratitude for having recovered from an illness. It houses a wooden statue of Santo Niño. (Niño is Spanish for "child.) Traditionally, pilgrims leave children's shoes there. They are given to the Christ child so that He will have new shoes as He travels the world on his mission to bring hope and comfort to us all. The second chapel houses a miraculous cross and in an adjoining room is the holy dirt. A prayer room is crowded with discarded canes and crutches that those who've been healed have left behind.

Today, the site looks very different from how it did in 1929 when the Archdiocese took possession of it. It sat on relatively high ground but the river flowed below, and over the course of time the forces of erosion had undermined the ground. The priest, Father Casimiro Roca, who viewed it in its dilapidated state supposedly responded by evoking Jesus' words "Truly I tell you, if you have faith as small as a mustard seed, you can say to this mountain, 'Move from here to there,' and it will move. Nothing will be impossible for you." (Matthew 17:20)

Undeterred by the size of the task, Father Roca went to local businessmen in nearby Espanola. Restoring the mission would literally mean taking dirt from a nearby mountain to shore up the structure. He asked them if they had faith. They said that they did. He told them that he wanted them to be true to their word. Weeks later, the businessmen organized construction crews to move more than 150 tons of dirt behind El Santuario de Chimayó to preserve it. When Father Roca asked the men what the work would cost, they told him that a few bottles of altar wine would do! For the next forty years Father Roca remained at the sanctuary, greeting pilgrims who'd heard of its healing powers.

Patricia added, "Many times in the Gospels Jesus says that it was a person's faith and not Him who healed their afflictions. He doesn't say, 'I have healed you.' In the same way that was what Father Roca was saying. It wasn't the dirt itself. It wasn't him. It's their faith. And that begs the question: What is faith? Faith is a gift that we receive. You have to be open. . . . You may not be healed but you may receive peace. And whatever you receive is the presence of God."

Whether we are Christian, Jewish, or Muslim, members of each faith have locations that allow believers to be better in touch with the wellspring of their faith. As Jesus told Thomas, blessed are those who don't need to see or to experience in order to believe. But He still mercifully let Thomas see and touch to believe. That's why we look for places where we can walk, where we can contemplate, and where we can find our Lord, to discover entry points into a deeper walk with Him. We all have the same destination in mind, but the routes we can take are many, and God has chosen to place signposts all along each of them. Even better, we can offer our hand and our hearts to aid those we encounter along the way who are struggling and find inspiration in those who walk with a surety that we may not have. We each move, station to station, in this life.

Austin had a moment where had come full circle as he walked in the beautiful, unfiltered sunshine of New Mexico. The skies were a crisp blue. The snow gleamed white on the mountains. The trees had just begun to bud. "There was a quality to the air," he remembered. "Unmistakable. I'm a really logical-thinking kind of person, but I know when something's different. And there was something. There was a presence in the air . . . reflective of faith and of the Lord."

Just as he had when he was a boy, he was taking on a mighty task from his Father, and he could feel the importance and the weight of it.

The entirety of Austin's experience, from the stroke to the pilgrimage, has refreshed his gratitude to God and his passion for loving his neighbors. "Something happened that was much more powerful than just me. Strange as it sounds, that stroke gave me a boost . . . I'm so grateful for the Lord."

From the moment that Austin received an earthly mission from his dad to the moment when he walked the suffering path of his savior, Jesus, he has sought to fulfill his duties to God and to his neighbor faithfully. While he's taken some detours, he's back on the road now. Across his life he's learned to be contented and rest in God's power and presence.

"You know, I'm not gonna live forever and that's not the point," he said, summing up his experiences. "But I'm going to be satisfied and have fun and die with a real satisfied mind of having lived life really, really well."

Positive thinking isn't everything. But knowing what we know of God's mercy and power and care, if we decide that a day is going to be a good day, we may just find that the spirit of contentment which Austin found in the desert can exist wherever we are.

We often find the spark that ignites the light to illuminate even at times of personal darkness, at times when we're not specifically searching for it. At unexpected times and in surprising ways, we are shown the power of faith and prayer. We may not set out determinedly on a pilgrimage. Sometimes the steps we take in service of one duty lead us to moments of real enlightenment, ones that lift mind and spirit. Sometimes the image and likeness of what we think we need doesn't come in the shape we thought it should.

In 2018, I traveled to Jerusalem to cover the opening of the US embassy in that ancient city. One afternoon, I had a few hours to take my own spiritual walk. I found myself strolling across the glistening marble of the courtyard in City of David. My steps led me to the Wailing Wall, a small segment of an ancient limestone retaining wall built to support the expansion of a Jewish temple. It is considered to be the holiest place where Jews can pray. It is also a site holy to Muslims, a place where the Prophet Muhammad tied his winged horse before he ascended to paradise.

I watched as Jews stood facing the wall, praying silently and bowing their heads. Some, as tradition dictates, slipped notes into the wall's cracks and crevices to ask for God's intercession. I was deeply moved and God's spirit emanated throughout the space. It wasn't just the wall that produced the calm in me. I had recently lost my mother and though I knew that she had gone on to a better place I missed her. She was my rock, my fortress, my foundation on which I had built my life, the woman who, along with my father, had lived a life that demonstrated the power of prayer. With her loss, I'd endured the greatest heartbreak of my life. Yet, through her, through the communion of prayer among that group of people unknown to me but known through our desire for comfort and a sign, I felt my faith deepening and my love for the Lord growing stronger.

People.

Places.

Prayer.

Peace.

We can learn a lot from suffering. Our society chooses to hide it away, pretending that it doesn't exist. The people in these stories know that it does. They know God has the power to overcome it. But they also know, as Paul wrote, that "suffering produces perseverance; perseverance, character; and character, hope." (Romans 5:3)

Healing

WHEN DANI MET DOUG

Miracles unfold in God's timing, not ours.

For it is by grace you have been saved, through
faith—and this is not from yourselves, it is the gift
of God—not by works, so that no one may boast.

—EPHESIANS 2:8–9

"This is real. This is real. This is real."

As Dani Laurion walked down the aisle of St. Mary Cathedral in Lansing, Michigan, her words were halting but her footsteps sure. Streetlights shone through the stained-glass windows in the clerestory, piercing the shadows over the evening service. Behind Dani, her husband, Doug, stood with his arms outstretched to catch her if she fell. Her mother, Linda, followed the couple, pushing the empty wheelchair that Dani had used for the past thirteen years.

"This is real," Dani repeated over and over, her words stronger with each of the first unaided steps she'd taken in all that time.

Her words no longer carried the hint of a question; they'd been transformed into a declaration.

If this were a Hollywood film, the instrumental music would begin to swell. Instead the sound of Brandon Lake's "Too Good to Not Believe," accompanied her walk.

Doug alternately pointed to his wife and raised his hands to the heavens as tears streamed down his face. An enormous smile illuminated Dani's face. Instead of carrying a portable ventilator attached to a tracheostomy tube, her hands were now raised in praise to God. She felt light. She felt free. "I used to feel like I was created from leftover pieces. I had that feeling for all of my life." The burden of a thought that had haunted her for her entire life was lifted. She kept walking toward the altar.

On March 15, 2022, Dani had raised her hands to God. "I just put my hands up and I just asked God to hold me."

God had answered her prayer. Hours after the healing service led by Dr. Mary Healy, Dani wasn't just walking, she bounded up the steps of Doug's son's home to share the good news. The next morning, the always energetic woman was bouncing up and down on the couple's bed. Dr. Healy had heard words of knowledge that late winter evening. The promises of spring had come early for the Laurions. In a month, the couple would walk together from their apartment in downtown Lansing to attend Easter Mass to celebrate the risen Lord.

THIRTEEN YEARS EARLIER, APRIL 23, 2009, in a hospital room in northern Michigan, nursing staff helped Dani rise to a seated position. They then assisted her to her feet. She stood unsteadily for a moment before her eyes rolled back and she blacked out.

Thirty-two-year-old Dani hadn't been feeling well for a few

days and was eventually hospitalized with pneumonia. She was generally very healthy. She was an avid scuba diver and had traveled widely to pursue her interest. She had a career she loved. She had an active social life. She was dating a man in a very caring relationship. She was looking forward to a bright future with little thought that it might be dimmer.

Her condition grew worse, and she was placed on a ventilator to aid her labored breathing. As Dani remembers it, "I was in a bed, and I woke up. The staff came in and turned the vent off. They got me to stand up. I immediately passed right out. So they tried it again. The same thing happened."

A series of tests revealed that Dani suffered from postural orthostatic tachycardia syndrome (POTS). As Doug, a veteran nurse, explained, "POTS is an autoimmune disease that causes her blood pressure to drop and her heart rate to go up when she tries to stand."

Dani was told that she would have to remain primarily in a wheelchair for the rest of her life. She would no longer be able to care completely for herself independently. She was discharged to a nursing home. She was thirty-two years old. Long years of having to rely on home health aides awaited her.

"Initially, I was terrified," Dani said. "But I also tend to make the best out of things pretty quickly. I was very outgoing and started to make friends at the nursing home. At that first facility, I even started to teach people to sew and do other things. We also had scheduled activities. Some nights we spent out on the patio listening to music. Still, it was very, very hard."

Dani was decades younger than the majority of the nursing home residents. She wondered sometimes what her friends and contemporaries were doing on the nights when she was parked in a wheelchair among the mostly elderly residents. Sometimes her frustration over her situation grew too strong. "I'd call my parents and tell them, 'I'm going to a bus stop. I'm leaving here.' It was a very, very difficult way to live. I was in my early thirties, and my friends were dying. I'd grow close to people, and they'd die. I saw a lot of that."

At first she and her boyfriend were able to maintain their relationship. He'd visit her every day, and sometimes Dani was well enough for off-site visits to his place. Dani's health continued to be a problem. She had repeated bouts of pneumonia and lung infections. Spending her time in and out of hospitals and then longer stints in nursing homes took a toll on her social life. Visits from friends grew more sporadic and then diminished almost entirely. "A nursing home is not a place that a lot of people want to go to visit a friend. It's just the nature of the beast. I ended up quite alone except for my friends within the facilities."

Dani's romantic relationship ended. She made and lost more friends among the residents. Years passed, and outwardly Dani made the most of a bad situation. Inwardly, she despaired. After all, what else could she expect for herself? When she was a child, she'd had a vision that had profoundly affected her view of herself. "I'd never shared with anyone the vision I'd carried with me since I was a child," she said. "I could picture the moment of my creation. I saw the figure of God. He had his back to me, so I couldn't see his face. He was bending over a series of trunks of leftover pieces. And from those, he assembled me."

She had been created out of leftover pieces. Dani believed that she had been assembled from discards—bits that weren't good enough for anyone else. So when her health kept failing, she saw it as inevitable.

Dani had also endured another setback with her health. Her POTS had continued to worsen, and her breathing had deteriorated to the point that she had been given a tracheotomy. That had left her with a hole in her throat into which a plastic valve was inserted allowing exterior access for the ventilator she needed to provide sufficient oxygen.

In the fall of 2017, Dani moved into a room at the Medilodge of Capital Area. Located in South Lansing, it was more convenient to where her family, her parents and her two brothers lived. The move may have been beneficial in that regard, but in others it was more of the same. Call it an assisted living facility, a retirement community, or anything else, Dani was once again an outlier. Still, despite the age gap between herself and the other residents, she did everything in her power to fit in and make the most of it. Medilodge is a wonderful facility that provides many amenities and services, but other than members of the staff, Dani was again living with people far older than she.

One of those staff members was Doug Laurion, a nurse who worked in the long-term care unit.

"Dani entered my unit," Doug told me. "I only kind of saw her once in a while in her wheelchair. She participated frequently in the activities, and she had to travel down my hallway to get to the activity room. And one day, she had her oxygen on, and with the trach, she was producing a lot of white noise. I didn't even turn around. I knew it was her, and I said, 'Good morning, Miss Vader.' And she just cracked up laughing."

Dani said hello and continued down the hallway to the activity room.

Neither of them sensed it at the time, but they'd look back on it as their "meet cute moment" right out of a romantic comedy. We know how it goes: Boy meets girl. Boy loses girl. Will boy get girl back? That's where the drama resides.

In the moment, though, that *Star Wars*–inspired exchange was the spark that began a friendship. It was the "When Dani met Doug" moment.

As Doug puts it now, laughing sardonically, "It was very romantic." He went on to add, "That just started a friendly relationship that stayed very platonic. At that point we just kind of bonded over the quality of patient life. The facility was going through some changes. We didn't have an activity director."

Dani was taking an active role to fill that void, and she wanted to ensure that the residents had some input into how the quality of life at Medilodge could be optimized.

"I had always heard that Doug was an exceptional nurse and that he would occasionally assist the activities coordinator and sometimes participate. He was the only one who really did that. I wanted to talk with someone seriously about how things should run there."

In the spring of 2018, the two agreed to meet for a discussion about care at Medilodge on one of Doug's days off. Years later, Dani's impish sense of humor and love of the man who would become her husband are evident. "I was so happy because he had scheduled this appointment. He came in that day, and he was dressed very nicely. He had his little briefcase with him, and he treated the discussion very seriously. That made me a happy young lady."

She was quick to clarify, "Doug became a very good friend of mine, a work friend in a way. The idea of me being in love with anyone was very, very far away in my mind. It wasn't that I thought poorly of myself, but I was realistic. I had a hole in my throat and these other things wrong with me, nobody is going to, you know, fall in love with it. And so I just decided that I was okay with it. Anything to do with love is very, very off my chart."

Doug's sense of humor shines through in his version of the events. He and Dani had become friends, and through her, he met her mother and other members of her family. All of them bonded over the University of Michigan Wolverine football team. Dani's eight-year-old niece, Sydney, was one of the biggest fans and always greeted Doug in the cutest way. At one point, they were all planning to attend one of the most long-standing and fiercest rivalry games in all of college football: the annual November showdown between the Wolverines and the Ohio State Buckeyes.

Laughing, Doug said, "East Lansing is the home of the Michigan State Spartans, so there aren't a lot of Wolverine fans around. I was pretty excited to find someone whose family was going to host a real Michigan tailgate party and had great tickets to the biggest game of the season."

In a way, Dani and Doug's spontaneous connection was years in the making. It takes a special kind of person to go into health care. That's especially true of those who work in geriatric care. By 2018, Doug had spent nearly all of his more than thirty years in nursing in that field.

"I grew up with a Catholic father and an Episcopalian mother," he said. "I went to public school but attended CCD [Confraternity of Christian Doctrine] classes and received the sacraments. I was very active in youth groups and young adult groups. There were several lay pastors who were mentors of mine."

Doug was the youngest in the family, and by the time he was born, his parents were nearly forty and his grandparents were well into their seventies. Combine that with a father who was an insurance agent who struggled as a salesperson because his focus was more on what his clients needed rather than his commissions, and Doug was right out of central casting for a life devoted to the welfare of others, in particular the elderly. In his nursing career he headed up wound clinics but spent most of his time in geriatrics. Health care professionals, as the ongoing COVID-19 pandemic has shown, are particularly subject to stress and trauma. It takes a special type of person to work with the elderly, whether it's in general geriatrics, palliative care, or hospice. The end stages of people's lives are when they need others most, but people often distance themselves from the aged and the dying.

"I stayed in it, but I saw a lot of people get burnout. It was hard to get close to people and then be saddened and affected by their loss," Doug said. "When somebody is dying, you can just go on the journey with them for a while. Hold their hand. Make them feel comfortable. Most important for me is that I reminded them that there was a place after this life that they would be going to. It wasn't in my job description, but addressing their spiritual needs and not just their physical ones. That's why I always looked at nursing as a vocation and not merely an occupation."

Doug explained this spiritual connection another way: "I've been with people when their physical life comes to an end. I've seen the beautiful process when the soul has been released from the body. When the soul is ready to go, there's just a tremendous peace that comes into the room. The door to the Kingdom opens. Two of the most beautiful experiences I had weren't at work. First was being with my own father when he passed after having a stroke. He ended up having another major stroke, and he went into a semicomatose state. Being with him, sitting vigil with him without the responsibility of having to be a nurse, was just such a peaceful moment for my siblings and me. The second happened very recently with my mother. Both Dani and I were bedside with her when she was called. Both those experiences served as a reminder of our union. It reminded me that we are all threads in a beautiful tapestry. I get to experience their life and their death as they move on to the next phase of life."

Dani's father had gone to Sacred Heart Major Seminary in Detroit to become a priest. He spent eight years there but was never ordained. He had left the seminary and married Dani's mother. He had exchanged one type of service for another. The family lived in Waterford, Michigan, a town thirty-eight miles north of Detroit and ninety-one miles southeast of Lansing, and he served as an officer in the Bloomfield Township Police Department.

"We went to church every week, and I don't think we ever missed more than two times," Dani said. "When we did, we had a family meeting to point out how God would understand. We were at church all the time, but there wasn't a real strong carryover from Sunday into the rest of the week. My idea of being a Catholic as a child was to sit there and be quiet, making sure that I stood straight and remembering to pray before and after every meal. I remember Catechism class, and it seemed more like it was about standing in a straight line and less about your experience with God. I think that was in large part because God wasn't talked about in the public schools and in society in general."

Dani realizes now that that's not what Catholicism truly is, but that was her perception as a child. As an adult, as you will see, her more mature perspective and experiences are much different. That transition began when she moved to Cheboygan, Michigan, and lived in a nursing home there around 2012. She went to a church run by Franciscan priests, the order founded by St. Francis of Assisi, the medieval saint commonly known for being the patron saint of animals. In a way, that connection to nature and animals was what reconnected Dani to the best religious experiences she'd had as a child.

"My favorite day of the year was Good Friday. As a family, we would get together, take the Bible, and go to the park to take turns reading passages from it. We'd sit by the water, and it was very serene and very beautiful. I held on to those images for years. Later, when I was living in Cheboygan, I'd go and visit the National Shrine of Cross in the Woods."

There, a number of religious sculptures, including one of St. Francis, stand in a beautiful natural sanctuary. What most moved Dani then, and continues to, is the sculpture *The Man on the Cross*. It is a twenty-eight-foot-tall statue of Jesus on the cross, just at the moment when, in Luke 23:46, "Jesus called out with a loud voice, 'Father, into your hands I commit my spirit.' When he had said this, he breathed his last." The artist said he had wanted to "give the face an expression of great peace and strength and offer encouragement to everyone who viewed the Cross."

Understandably, Christ's last breath would resonate strongly with someone who has struggled to breathe for so long. Dani remains in awe of the beauty of the place and also fondly recalls those Good Friday trips as a child. She can see now that "that was the only real time I felt like my religion turned into my faith."

That same transformation occurred at the shrine and at the parish in Indian River. "While I was there was when I really listened to more of the words that the priest was preaching. I started to read the Bible more. I read more religious-themed books. I started to feel a strong attachment to God. I can't really say that

I felt like I do today, but I was moving much closer to where I eventually ended up."

The National Shrine of the Cross in the Woods was Dani's parish, and there she served as a youth group leader. She also sat on the Pastoral Council. "Father Mike Haney was very warm and a great teacher. My experience there was the true beginning of a deeper, more intimate faith."

Dani's miracle healing was still years away, but the path to it began long before 2022. Time and again we see this story arc. We sometimes hear the phrase "spontaneous healing," but in fact, miracles like the one Dani was given have very long roots that are often invisible even to those on whom the gift was bestowed.

Along with feeling a stronger attachment to God, Dani and Doug were increasingly drawn to each other. Due to a downturn in her health, Dani and Doug weren't able to attend that Michigan versus Ohio State football game in November 2018. Dani was hospitalized, and Doug gave up the prime seat he'd been offered at the stadium in Ann Arbor for another seat—in Dani's hospital room. She'd been stepped down from an intensive care unit, and he visited her at the hospital. The two refer to that evening as "bedgate." Doug showed up with food suitable for a tailgate party—sausages and cheeses—and he sat along side Dani on the bed as they ate and watched the game.

Then something happened. Dani said, "At some point, Doug put his hand on my knee. And all of a sudden, my heart totally flipped and flopped. And the idea of never having love in my life, and then 'Oh, my gosh, what's going on? And I thought 'Could it be? Oh my gosh, I think it is.' And I thought, 'I don't know for sure, but I'm never moving my leg again.'"

That Dani found hope at that particular moment was especially significant. She'd just learned that, having been on and off ventilators since 2009, she was now going to have to be on one overnight every night. As difficult as it was to have spent the previous nine years in and out of nursing homes, in assisted living situations, and living among people mostly forty years older than herself, she was now, as Doug put it, "learning just how small her world was going to be. Life and her condition were closing down on top of her. She just wasn't seeing any hope."

Doug's sense of her despair was signaled by something Dani revealed to him the same night as "bedgate." She told him about the vision she'd had in her childhood—the image of herself created as some freak show experiment, out of discarded bits. Doug listened. But then he asked her, "Did you ever see his face?"

Dani considered. "I immediately saw that image again. His back was to me the entire time. When Doug asked me that, I knew that answer immediately. I knew that Doug knew the answer." She had never seen the face of the figure in her dream that was carelessly creating her out of rubbish.

Doug told her that the image of the man wasn't God. It was Satan.

"My knowledge of God, my belief of God suited everyone but me," Dani recalled. "I always believed that I was separate from everyone else. Different. That's how I saw my creation, why I was put together from parts that God wouldn't use on anyone else. I also felt like I deserved this life, my medical issues. I was getting exactly what I was supposed to be getting. Actually, I thought I was getting less than that. I was an experiment, and I shouldn't have lived as long as I had. I had expected that my life would have been over years before."

Doug saw something in his mind's eye as well: "I started casting a new vision for Dani. I saw the need to test out a new vision of life for her. Following that bedgate night and learning that Dani had to be on a vent full-time each night, we started to talk to respiratory therapists. We discussed how small the machines can be. We heard stories about how people with them lived their lives. They could work. They could have full lives. And as we heard those words, I started seeing myself in that kind of life with her. As Dani realized that she could do more, I got it, too. We could do more together."

Things wouldn't be easy, but the pair dealt with it. This time, together, they said in unison, "This is real."

In January 2019, Doug drove Dani to the home he was renting, and she moved in with him. On the last day of May of that year, they were engaged. In November 2019, they were married in a ceremony presided over by their best friend, Peter. Since Doug was divorced, they couldn't be married in the Catholic Church until some procedural matters were handled. Eventually the couple had those issues sorted, and in December 2021, in front of thirty friends as part of a regular Mass, they exchanged wedding vows again.

By then they had moved into an apartment in downtown Lansing. It had an elevator and easy access to the library, restaurants, shops and, more critically, to St. Mary Cathedral. Dani and Doug began to attend Mass regularly.

Doug recalled, "It was a huge step for us to come back to the church and get our marriage blessed. We were at Mass with all our friends and family. There was a beautiful service. Reverend Karl Pung, who said Mass and presided over our saying vows, had been very dear to us throughout our time at St. Mary. He had such a positive impact on our life in so many ways. Going to Mass was no longer an obligation but something we looked forward to. Father spoke of joy and love. Loving God was his central message. He is an incredible teacher and a true shepherd of God. One Sunday I saw in the church bulletin a notice for an adult welcome group. A woman named Theresa invited us to attend. The people were very welcoming, and we also learned that it served as a prayer group." They prayed over Dani, and after the second time Dani and Doug attended the group, Doug began to feel that God wanted to heal her.

Dani was facing another health crisis. At the end of 2021, she was told that her trachea was in the early stages of collapse. The cartilage that normally holds the trachea open was failing. That was probably a result of her having had a tracheostomy for so long. A diagnosis of excessive dynamic airway collapse was then followed by the even more frightening-sounding tracheomalacia and tracheobronchomalacia. She was able to inhale independently of a respirator, but she couldn't exhale without one. Having to use one 24/7 was problematic. Being confined to a bed is one thing; trying to live a more active life while attached to a respirator was another. At various times the hose came out of the connector. Panic would set in immediately and subside a bit only after Doug reattached it.

"It was a very hard time. Just very scary," Dani said.

In the face of those difficulties, attending prayer group was another challenge, not just physically but because of facing a new experience. "That was the first time that I was exposed to praying out loud in a small group like that," Dani said. "I'd recited prayers at Mass, but that was mostly sticking to script. I'd say a Hail Mary, an Our Father, or say the rosary. This was very different. People prayed with their own words, their own feelings, their own heart. It was beautiful. Father Karl had done the same thing with us a few times. I relied so much on his teaching and learned so much from him. It kind of blew my mind in a way because I always thought it would be wonderful to pray like that. I did talk to God, but I didn't nurture that part of my experience because in my mind it wasn't praying. I was also still stuck a bit in my thinking that God was watching over us from a distance. We didn't have a personal relationship with Him. He was all powerful but kind of distant. I was gradually coming to see that wasn't the case. I loved praying with other Catholics, and it was a new but beautiful experience, and then at one of those sessions someone told me that they'd received a sense that God wanted me to ask someone for forgiveness. That was very, very odd to me. I'd never had someone tell me that they'd gotten the sense that God was communicating with them that way."

Dani didn't pray to God to heal her at those group sessions or at other times. Mostly she asked for forgiveness. She and her brother had a distant relationship. Among all the family members, he was the one with whom she had the worst relationship. She felt that he looked down on her. She believed that she couldn't live up to his standards. They barely acknowledged each other's existence and could find nothing in common to talk about. As siblings they had loved each other, but they had never connected personally.

Dani prayed about her brother and asked God for forgiveness. If she hadn't been prompted to by that member of the prayer group, she likely wouldn't have.

Two weeks prior to Dani's miraculous unaided walk to the front of the church, Dani and Doug heard that Dr. Mary Healy would be doing a three-night presentation on healing. The couple decided to attend. The first two nights, Dr. Healy, a professor of Sacred Scripture at Sacred Heart Major Seminary in Detroit, spoke. A highly regarded expert in Scripture, evangelism, healing, and the spiritual life, she conducted the sessions and would also hold a healing service on the last night.

Dani recalled, "She talked about prayer. She talked about the importance of forgiveness. She talked about the importance of feeling worthy to receive forgiveness. She also talked a lot about healing as it occurs in Scripture. I was glad that she also emphasized that she didn't consider herself a 'healer.' She said that God does the healing; she just teaches us about it."

If it weren't for Dr. Healy's explanation that she wasn't a healer, Dani says that she wouldn't have attended the healing service. "My idea of healers was formed by what I saw on television. You know, people coming forward and being smacked on the forehead and falling backward, that kind of thing. I just had no concept of what that service was going to be like. I understood intellectually all the concepts that Dr. Healy had talked about the first two nights. It all made complete sense. But that service was a real unknown."

Dani was especially drawn to the notion of forgiveness, letting go of things, and feeling that she was beyond God's forgiveness. On the Sunday before the healing service, she had prayed about the situation with her brother. She forgave him in her own heart for what he had done that had made her feel wronged. That same Sunday, despite whatever misgivings or anxiety she had about the healing service, she joined Julie Becka, the coordinator of Youth Ministry at the church. In addition, Julie is a member of the prayer group. Julie planned to take the members of the Youth Ministry out onto the streets of Lansing. Their mission was to invite members of the public to attend the healing service. Dani decided to join them.

"I had a wonderful morning watching those kids live their faith. It was really beautiful to see them talking to so many different people. At one point, a very nice looking man came along, and the kids invited him. He stopped and said that his father had been a minister and he'd witnessed some healing in his own home. He then said that he was going to join us that night."

Dani invited her parents, and her mother agreed to join them. Her father, a Parkinson's disease patient, wasn't able to attend. Doug was working that day and would arrive sometime after the service started at seven o'clock. Dani and her mother settled into the thirteenth row. Dani recalled, "I had walked into the healing service with some hope in my heart. I didn't know what to expect. It was a healing service, and I thought anything could happen. I was more nervous than anything. This was all so new to me."

The music began, and just to her right was the nice-looking man who'd said he would show up. "I was sitting there, and I could see that, like me, he was really enjoying the music. He was joining in the singing. It was clear to me that man was just joyful. He was filled with the spirit, and any thought I had about the healing service maybe having something to do with me went right out the window. I was just so happy for that man and how happy he was. Subconsciously, I suppose it was easier for me to think that the healing was for him and not for me. Everybody else there seemed so comfortable, but I still had no idea how things were going to proceed."

Doug arrived and sat with Dani and her mother. Dr. Healy spoke about healing, faith, and prayer. At one point, Dani noticed some of those in attendance spontaneously raising their hands toward Heaven. Dr. Healy remarked on that and said that when you're moved to raise your hands in that manner, you should think of doing what you did as a child: holding your arms up and asking for your father to pick you up.

"I did what Dr. Healy said, I put my hands up in the air. And as if God was my father and I was a little girl, I asked him to please hold me, to keep me, and to take care of me." Instantly, the rest of her surroundings faded. God was standing in front of her, reaching out to help her. She immediately felt that He was going to take care of her. "And I saw God, and He looked just like any of the other men in the church. He could have been a neighbor or a friend. He looked so approachable, so much like just any of us. Then I felt as if water was being poured in both my ears."

Dani turned to Doug, "Do you think I should take off my vent?"

Doug wasn't sure.

Dr. Healy said to the assembled, "I have a word of knowledge that someone's lungs are being reinflated."

Doug looked at Dani and said, "Go ahead."

Dani disconnected from the vent. "I took my first breath. In. Out. Then I did it again. By the fourth time, I realized that I was fine. Everything was going on in my mind at once. It was kind of like I was in a dream, except in a dream there's always something that doesn't quite fit the scene. Those things remind you that you're dreaming. None of that happened. Everything I saw, everything I heard, everything I felt was real."

Dani was crying. Her mother reached over to Dani to console her. She thought that Dani's tears were tears of disappointment and not stunned amazement and gratitude. The trio sat there stunned, dumbstruck. As Dani continued to inhale and exhale normally, her mother noticed that her daughter was fine and no longer connected to the life-giving ventilator.

The three of them were focused on one another. Then they heard "If anyone has been healed, we'd like you come up to the altar and share your story."

Doug stood up to allow Dani to scoot over to the aisle. Her mother stepped around Dani and spread the wheelchair so her daughter could sit in it and make her way to the altar to share her remarkable story of having her breathing restored. Linda quietly followed Dani with the chair as she walked up the aisle. She thought at first that Dani was experiencing the effects of an adrenaline surge.

That was when Dani's "This is Real" procession began.

Doug walked behind her, gradually realizing the truth of his wife's words.

This is real.

Linda realized that Dani wasn't going to collapse into a heap. This is real.

Not only is Dani's healing real and miraculous, it is lasting. She continues to walk independently and easily. Her stair-taking, bed-jumping abilities have not diminished in the slightest. Nor have her spirit and her gratitude. Immediately following the healing service, Dani and Doug spoke privately with Dr. Healy and Father Karl. He assured them that God had given Dani that gift with no strings attached. They didn't owe God anything. Given their individual and collective past and their approach to life, Dani and Doug want to continue to be of service. For them, it is still early days, and they are not yet sure exactly what that will mean for them. They want to share, and in various ways have shared, their story. They want it to continue to be a source of inspiration and hope. They want it to serve as a beacon of light in what has been for all of us a dark time.

When asked why it is that God chose to heal her that night, Dani said, "In part, we received this healing because I was open to it, because I asked for it. Because for the first time I asked God to take all of it from me, I didn't pray for something small and help with a little something. I prayed. I just prayed big. An incredible mentor of mine, Bill Lewis, taught me the importance of doing that. . . . And then Doug and I believe that it's important to share that we each have a lot of things in our past that we're not proud of. We would love to be able to turn back time to change some things, but we can't and we won't. And we wouldn't because this is who we are right now as who God wants us to be and who he created. So the good, the bad, the ugly, all of it together makes us who we are right now. And everything that made me could receive the healing from God. It's there for anyone. It is there for anyone and for everyone. I don't know how God will decide who receives it. But if we're not willing and we're not ready, then I don't believe we would receive it."

Doug added, "You know, more than ever, especially living right downtown in an area that's rife with homeless, you see the people who need God's healing. If we were to think that all is right in the world because things have improved so much in our lives, then what's the point of the miracle? And we just are really moved with the compassion to go about figuring out how we can bring God into people's lives so that they can know Him. So that they can know Him like we know Him and experience Him like we've experienced Him."

Dani elaborated on Doug's point: "The other day, somebody

asked me if my world was different. I said, 'The world is the same. Our perspective and our role in this world has drastically changed. This is the Kingdom of God. Many people want to deny His existence. Yet He is everything. The world is the same, and we still see homeless people in the street. Now we truly see that individual as a child of God. The same as you!'"

And as far as Dani feeling broken and an assemblage of discarded parts? "I was never broken. My thoughts? My ideas? They were a bit broken. I was never physically broken. And for people out there in the world that feel like that, I want to be helpful to show them that same God is there with them. That vision I had before of a man standing with his back to me? That wasn't God. The figure whose face I saw and who was so warm and welcoming? That was God."

God is real.

What Doug and Dani experienced was no movie script. It was a case of a real, active, compassionate, and caring God answering prayers in His time. Dani raised her hands to God as a child would do in asking a father to take care of His child.

This kind of relationship with God is amazing grace.

Dani put it best: "As Christians everywhere, the peace and the power of God is within us all. . . . God does not heal as a side gig. God is a healer!"

HOW COVID-19 SAVED A LIFE

Holding onto faith through a pandemic of disease and fear.

> But when you ask, you must believe and not doubt,
> because the one who doubts is like a wave of the
> sea, blown and tossed by the wind.
>
> —JAMES 1:6

Nine-year-old Lisa braced her shoulders and straightened her church dress. Unafraid and full of purpose, she started the long march down the sanctuary of First Baptist Church in Douglas, Georgia, feeling the eyes of the congregation on her.

It was a special occasion. Lisa was being baptized.

She was required to give a profession of faith before the church. Alone, without the peer pressure of her friends, little Lisa had decided this was the moment.

"I wasn't scared or anything. I just knew I was supposed to do it," she remembers now. Even at nine, she knew her own mind and knew what God was saying to her.

And she was always comfortable putting her life in His hands. From the time she was born and began attending First Baptist Church, Lisa had a second home there. "Every time the doors to the church opened, we were there."

That day, stepping into the warm water, Lisa felt an overwhelming sense of how special she was.

Fast-forward forty years. Marriage. Kids. A career of teaching that she loved. Through it all Lisa felt God's faithfulness again and again. Yet suddenly she found herself in a scenario she hadn't anticipated—one where she wasn't sure at all where she was supposed to be.

And without warning she was having thoughts of a heartbreaking, adult prayer. "I often prayed to God that I would die."

A DEVOUT CHRISTIAN, LISA MARTIN, at age forty-nine, knew that she would never actually take her own life. Instead, she asked God to do it. Lisa and her husband, Jeff, had raised four upstanding young adults. Lisa had enjoyed a rewarding teaching career. Jeff had successfully transitioned from a life as a pastor to that of a successful business owner and operator. The family seemingly had everything they could want or need, including a loving extended family and circle of friends.

Still, Lisa mysteriously felt abandoned. "I felt I could die. None of them would care if I weren't around," she said. She wondered what had happened. Why had so many things in her life changed? Why was it that others didn't need her as they once had? The innocence and certainty of the childhood Lisa were gone.

That certainty would come back. God would prove to Lisa that she was loved and valued. He'd show her how much she'd underestimated her own value. But it would take a crisis that would bring her closer to the brink than she'd ever been.

CHILDREN LEAVING THE HOUSE FOR the last time is often a bittersweet experience for parents. They may be glad to abandon the role of chauffeur, hustling to get the kids to various activities. They may be proud of their children's accomplishments and their growing maturity but still miss being depended upon as nurturers. An empty nest is often disconcerting for that very reason.

In 2020, Lisa Martin began feeling aimless and useless when her daughters and her son were no longer living in the house. The three girls, Madison, Harper Lee, and Natalie, had all moved out, and Jackson was attending college. Jeff was heavily involved in running five different businesses. Lisa started to feel misunderstood. She believed that her friends and family members had turned away from her. She was a language arts teacher who said of her work, "I love teaching. I mean, there's just nothing else I would have rather done. I mean that." Yet despite how much she loved her work, she was no longer teaching. She'd taken a job in an associated field in education, but it wasn't as fulfilling as her previous job had been.

For years, she had wondered, what would she do when she could no longer teach? When her own children no longer really needed her as they once did, when her husband seemed to her to be more interested in his work than in their life together. What would she do then? The future stretched out in front of her, a vast, undiscovered territory, mysterious and menacing.

These are questions we all face at points in our lives. We put so much of our self-worth into being successful, wanted, needed. If your whole identity is being a giver, having nothing left to give can seem like having no reason left to live.

All those questions haunted her in September 2020.

Jeff knew that his wife was unhappy, but at the time, he wasn't fully aware of the depth of her feelings. She confided her inner-most thoughts and feelings about her death wish only to God and to her younger brother, Parker. She wanted to make certain that if God answered her prayer by having her die by accident or illness, no medical intervention would interfere with God's plan for her. "I went and updated my will. I made a living will. I said that I didn't want to be resuscitated. At the time I didn't know what a ventilator was. I figured that if I got some disease, it would be ten years or so before I would need to even think about those kinds of things."

Lisa was wrong about how people felt about her. She was wrong about the void that she thought her life had become. But she wasn't wrong about getting ill. The choices she made in filing a living will were about to come into play. Within months, ravaged by COVID-19, Lisa lay in a hospital bed in a coma. Her family was nearby, as close as quarantine regulations would allow. The clock was ticking. That ventilator she didn't know much about? The family had decided to keep her on it for eleven more days. The ventilator was keeping her alive; her body had shut down. They told the family it was only a matter of time.

The matter was left in God's hands.

A SELF-DESCRIBED VERY DECISIVE PERSON, Lisa never doubted her feelings or questioned her decision about making the commitment to be baptized so young. "I never questioned it. I have been faithful ever since."

She's also faithfully listened when God guided her. She met her future husband when she was six years old and he was eight. She remembers when she was fifteen years old, and she was descending the stairs and she heard a whispering that told her she would marry Jeff.

"Now I know it was a God whisper. That was my very, very, very first recollection of God actually speaking to me. There have been other times. I've heard women talking about how when they're expecting a child, they feel a fluttering in their stomach, lot of butterfly wings. That's what I feel in my mind when God is speaking to me. It comes out of nowhere."

Lisa and Jeff are both accustomed to turning to God for His guidance. Prior to getting married, Jeff told Lisa that he believed that he was supposed to enter the ministry. Lisa was fine with that. She was a youth director at her church. She sang in the choir. She performed with an all-female Gospel group. Her faith was strong and steadfast. She accepted Jeff's calling at his word. Jeff wanted greater certainty. They had been married for nearly three years. She was teaching, and Jeff was working for his father. He had graduated with a degree in broadcasting. The field was highly competitive, the openings few, and Jeff used that fact as a means to test his belief in the rightness of his sense that the ministry was the right path for him to pursue. He didn't want to commit to it, though, unless he received some sign from God that this truly was His calling.

At the start of the year, Jeff devised a plan. If he received a call from a television producer offering him a job, he would turn down the offer, knowing that God had sent a sign that the ministry was his true path. To prevent anyone from manipulating the plan, Jeff told only his wife and their pastor. One July evening, the young couple sat out on deck of their new home, listening to the crickets and the moth wings fluttering against the porch light. The phone rang. Lisa rose to answer it. The man on the line introduced himself. He was from a local affiliate, and he wanted to speak to Jeff about a job. In recalling that night, Lisa choked up recalling those moments: "It was strange that the man explained everything to me without even asking to speak to Jeff directly. When I heard that God had delivered the message through me, I dropped the phone! I just yelled to Jeff, 'You got your calling!' And he looked at me, puzzled. 'Okay, who is it?' I knew he was confused, and said, 'No, no, Jeff, I said, you have got your calling!'"

Jeff picked up the phone and introduced himself. The man again explained why he had phoned. Jeff listened to him and thanked him. He then explained what had just transpired and that God had just used the man as a conduit to deliver the message to Jeff. Lisa also believes that God had the man explain everything to her first so that she would believe that God's confirming message of the rightness of Jeff's desire was real.

"It was so undeniable that we walked away from everything. We quit our jobs, and we moved to Birmingham, Alabama, for Jeff to go to seminary school. It was so undeniably God who was reaching out to us that we were so filled with joy."

But God's sign also indicated a significant change in their lives. "I thought our life was planned out. We were going to stay in Douglas, Georgia, with our family for the rest of our lives. Jeff was going to take over the family business. We ended up leaving all our family and friends. We didn't have a lot of money saved up, but we were able to buy a house in Birmingham. We had just enough money to get by while Jeff was in seminary school. The colors in the interior of the house matched everything we had bought previously. We didn't have to buy much at all. God provides what we need when we need it in the way we need it." Their savings lasted just long enough for him to graduate from seminary school. By that time, they were the proud parents of three daughters.

In the oddest way, money and Jeff's future were entwined in another way just as he was about to graduate. Like many graduates, Jeff fretted about whether or not anyone would want his services. He needn't have worried. Seven different churches were interested in having him serve as a minister. They all seemed to be great opportunities, even the ones that were farther from their family in Georgia. One day Jeff came to her and said, "I had a dream, and in it there was something about a 1972 US quarter. I'm convinced that somehow our decision about which church we decide to go to is going to involve a '72 quarter."

Lisa thought that was a bit crazy, but she went along with it. They continued to visit different churches, where they met the selection committee and Jeff preached. Each one seemed to be a great fit, and all Jeff asked in return for their offer was two weeks to consider it. "We kept looking for a '72 quarter to come about. We didn't know if we were going to see one on a billboard in town or how it would show up. But we were looking for that sign. We had family pressuring us to stay nearby to Douglas. But we wanted to be obedient. We wanted to go where God wanted us to go."

If they'd had their way, they would have accepted the offer from a church in nearby Waycross, Georgia. During the two weeks that Jeff was considering Waycross and waiting for a sign from God in the form of that '72 quarter, Lisa took the three girls shopping at a Winn-Dixie in Birmingham. When she went to pay, the clerk gave her change. She laid in the palm of Lisa's hands some bills and coins. Among them was a '72 quarter.

"I was the one who called Jeff. I said, 'You've got your call. God has answered, just like you said He would. That lady put a 1972 quarter in my hand.' And to this day, I have that 1972 quarter."

Given that context, it is easier to understand why, in her despair,

Lisa turned to God again, asking Him to end her life. Instead, God sent her a sign letting her know that she was truly loved.

BY THE START OF SEPTEMBER 2020, more than 190,000 people in the United States had died of COVID-19. By the beginning of the new year, that number would spike to more than 375,000. Lisa was very concerned and very vigilant about following the proper protocols to prevent the spread of the dangerous virus. Jeff was worried about supporting their kids and was pouring himself into work; he disagreed with Lisa about the seriousness of the virus. Lisa had other health matters on her mind. She had a cancer scare that added to the stress that we were all feeling as the pandemic took its toll. Then she had another. A mammogram revealed a sizable lump. She was told to schedule a needle biopsy as soon as possible. Into the gloom that colored her days emerged another vision: her death and release from the psychic pain that seemed so unrelenting.

"If I have cancer," she told Jeff, "I won't seek treatment. Just let me go. Why go through chemo and all the rest just that I might extend my life by a few months or a few years? I know where I'm going and to whom I belong."[52]

Jeff was concerned about his wife's mental and emotional state. He'd seen how it had deteriorated over time. He told her that he loved her and others cared about her. But it didn't seem to sink in.

Still, there were other matters to attend to. At that point, with the help of Harper Lee, they were running two businesses that were keeping them both very, very busy. At that point, Jeff wasn't in ministry anymore, but work still filled up his life. Despite Lisa's urging, Jeff hadn't strictly followed COVID-19 precautions at the offices, feeling that much of the concern about the pandemic was merely political posturing in an election year. He looked at the numbers and saw no real need to worry. A three-day cold, he assumed, wasn't reason to panic.

In mid-September, the bookkeeper Jeff employed fell ill and went to see a doctor. She tested positive for COVID-19. Her husband, who worked for Jeff as a part-time salesman, did, too. Jeff was upset. He'd have to shut down the offices. He and Harper Lee would have to be tested. They'd have to disinfect the offices. He and his daughter went to the clinic. His test came back positive; Harper Lee's did not.

When he reported the news to Lisa, she was infuriated. Getting tested wasn't the problem; needing to be tested was. All of this, she felt, could have been avoided if Jeff had been less stubborn in his thinking and worried more about their physical well-being than about their financial stability. Their differing beliefs about the value of work and about COVID-19 risk had reached a crisis point. The tension between them had grown palpable during the course of the pandemic. Now ironically, given what she had asked of God, her worst fear was being realized. She didn't think that COVID-19 would kill her, but what she and her husband would have to endure was a painful and unnecessary nuisance.

That same night, Lisa developed a slight fever. The couple isolated themselves. Harper Lee became their caregiver, remaining downstairs from her parents when not delivering what the couple needed. They planned to weather the storm by taking antibiotics, drinking as many fluids as possible, and showering frequently to keep their breathing airways open. Lisa deteriorated more rapidly. Her fever raged, and even a dunking in a cold outdoor pool did little to stem its rise. Jeff was strict about monitoring their vital signs. They were doing everything they could at home to manage their worsening condition.

Prior to that, Lisa had thought that she would be the one caring for her infected husband; instead, despite his weakened condition, he was the one who would have to tend to her. On September 26, Lisa managed to shout from the bedroom where she was isolated into the room where Jeff was isolated. She couldn't breathe. Her lungs hurt. Jeff managed to get out of bed to check on her. He told her that all she had to do was get through the night. In the morning he'd find some way to get supplemental oxygen bottles for them. He retreated to his room. Exhausted by the walk and the fever, he fell into a deep sleep.

Overnight, Lisa's condition worsened. She managed to get into the shower, but she could no longer stand. She slumped to the floor with the water spilling over her. She pounded on the wall, hoping to get Jeff's attention. With fans blowing to help cool him, he didn't hear her cries. Lisa remained in the shower, alternately sobbing and raging. Eventually, she got up enough strength to crawl from the bathroom to the bedroom. She found her phone and texted Jeff, "I need to go to the hospital!" She pressed "send" and waited. She waited until ten the next morning, when Jeff finally woke up.

What he saw frightened him. Lisa was struggling to breathe. Her fever had tinted her skin a deep red. Jeff checked her vital signs. Her temperature was dangerously high, her oxygen saturation dangerously low; her pulse was racing. A quick phone call to a physician friend got Jeff into motion. The doctor strongly recommended that Lisa be taken to hospital immediately. Jeff thought of their small regional medical center in Waycross but wanted to be assured that they'd get the best medical care, and that was ninety minutes away in either Jacksonville, Florida, or Savannah. His friend told him that they couldn't wait.

Lisa urged her husband to call an ambulance. He disagreed, saying he could get her there sooner. Jeff's friend recommended that they call the emergency room and advise them of Lisa's condition and her vitals. They couldn't risk being diverted to another hospital. The viral outbreak was raging in the area. Minutes might matter.

Lisa remembers little of the drive to the hospital and the many days after that. "I remember thinking to myself that if I were to die, I wanted to make certain that I was going to live with Jesus and then proclaimed, 'Lord, if I die today, I want to live with you. You are my Lord and Savior. I want to go to Heaven.'"[53] She didn't know that she was being held in the emergency room area instead of intensive care. The hospital was overwhelmed with COVID-19 patients. She'd have to wait to be moved. Jeff was only vaguely aware of how his wife was doing. He was still battling the disease himself. A doctor told him that the best thing he could do would be to take care of himself. He couldn't be of much use to Lisa in his present condition. No visitors were allowed, anyway. Jeff slowly improved, but focusing on Lisa's treatment plan and status remained difficult. The girls pitched in as best they could.

In the early stages of her battle, Lisa was advocating for herself as well. "While being wheeled into the makeshift room and while being hooked up to intravenous fluids, I demanded that I be hooked up to a ventilator. I must have said it at least five times. Until entering the ER, I had never even heard of the vent, yet there I was requesting and demanding to be placed on it. This

God-whispered request resulted in giving my family the time they needed to meet, discuss, and to determine a plan going forward."

Lisa didn't realize that for the vast majority of COVID-19 patients, being placed on a ventilator was nearly like receiving a death sentence. Many went on them; few recovered. Lisa was in critical condition, but her doctors were hopeful. She was only forty-nine years old, and despite the two cancer scares, she was in good health. Crucially, she'd never smoked, so her lungs, despite the infection, were in good shape. Still, her condition worsened. She struggled with the mask she wore, part of the noninvasive BiPAP machine that was being used to assist her breathing. She was nauseated and vomited frequently.

One of Lisa's nurses was Harper Lee's close childhood friend Hannah. She kept the family apprised of Lisa's condition and urged them to do everything they could to convince Lisa not to request the ventilator. Jeff texted Lisa, begging her to let go of the idea that seemed to have taken hold of her in her febrile state. She didn't respond to him. He wasn't certain if she understood the possible damage that being on a ventilator could do. Mucus could build up in the lungs, weakening them and hampering the body's healing mechanisms.

Jeff began posting on Facebook, hoping to get as many people as possible to pray for Lisa and to keep their friends and family informed. By October 1, what Jeff had feared and Lisa had asked for became their new reality. Doctors had determined that the best course of treatment was for Lisa to be placed on a ventilator. She was in a very weakened condition, but they believed that she was still strong enough to fight the virus. If they waited too long and her immune system became even more overwhelmed, that would no longer be the case. Though they didn't say it, Jeff had done his due diligence. If they waited too long to have her intubated and have her breathing taken over by the ventilator, Lisa would most likely become one of the 75 percent of ventilated COVID-19 patients who didn't survive.

Prior to the procedure, Lisa had been able to FaceTime with Jeff and three of the four kids. Madison was working with her students and couldn't join the meeting. A dedicated teacher herself, Lisa understood. Despite how weak she was, she was as upbeat as possible. The family was as well, encouraging her to continue to fight and stay strong. They all loved her and wished that circumstances could be different so that she could be by their side.

On the drive home, rain fell. Jeff cried and prayed, wondering what he would do if he lost his beloved wife. He wondered what he could do in the immediate moment to help her. Eventually, he answered the second of those questions. He would use that moment in time to bring God glory, no matter what the outcome might be. He also decided to journal the family's travails on Facebook more regularly, charting their ups and downs. He hoped that by doing so, other doubters about the seriousness of the devastating effects of the virus would take the pandemic more seriously. He also resolved to recover fully. He had yet to test negative for the virus. That meant that he was not allowed to visit Lisa. He had not laid eyes on her in person since September 27. He missed her deeply.

Finally, on October 5, feeling much better, Jeff got the good news he was hoping for: he was no longer infectious. As soon as he got the result, he drove to the hospital. Though he wasn't allowed into the room, he saw her through the glass partition in the intensive care unit. He was elated. Lisa seemed to be at peace. The staff at the hospital was supportive. They shared all the information they could about her condition, the medications being administered to her, and what the readout on the ventilator signaled. Jeff visited Lisa three times a day, at 8:00 a.m., 1:00 p.m., and 6:00 p.m. He resumed doing some work. Harper Lee had shouldered much of the burden of keeping their operations functional. Mindful of Lisa's feeling as though he had shunted her aside in focusing so much on work, he tried to strike a better balance. Time would tell how Lisa's disease and treatment would progress. He read widely about the virus and the disease it caused. He assembled a support team with whom he could share ideas and insights about COVID-19. In his role as a pastor, he had gone on numerous medical missionary excursions. He was comfortable interacting with doctors, knowing when he was nearing the limits of their patience.

Jeff's patience paid off. Eleven days after being placed on the ventilator, Lisa tested negative for the second time within the prescribed twenty-four-hour window.

Jeff and the kids were then allowed to be in the room with Lisa. He could hold her hand and kiss her for the first time in more than two weeks. Natalie came to the hospital and did her mama's nails. Madison showed up with a playlist of songs and lotion to soothe Lisa's skin. Lisa was heavily sedated, but Jeff knew from his pastoral care courses that even in that state, she could still hear. He put together his own list of songs on his phone. He placed it above her bed and let it loop over and over. He wanted to "surround her with the praise of God twenty-four hours a day."[54] Collectively, the family showered her with love and encouragement.

Because of their age, Lisa's parents had to remain in quarantine. Among Jeff's many tasks was keeping them apprised of their daughter's condition, texting them multiple times a day and phoning them as well. Jeff was aware that he needed and wanted to care for those who cared for and about his wife. He began to bring coffee and donuts for the hospital staff. He could see how anguished they were at having to deal with death and associated trauma on a scale none of them could have imagined when they had chosen healing and health as a profession. He suggested to the hospital administration that it find a chaplain to minister to their spiritual and emotional needs. All those acts of kindness and consideration in the middle of such pain, suffering, and stress were a balm. "As you give, so shall you receive" was in full effect in the halls and rooms of Memorial Satilla Health in Waycross, Georgia.

Many people who live in or near major metropolitan areas here in the United States take for granted the access they have to top-notch, state-of-the-art medical care. We don't think about our fellow citizens who live in rural areas where residents have no ready access to, or can even pay for, cutting-edge, emerging treatments. They may not even have access to information and the luxury of time that Jeff did to research the disease and the evolving best practices to treat critical cases like Lisa's. He became aware of a new treatment that could potentially increase Lisa's chances of getting off the ventilator and surviving. The problem was, the hospital in Waycross wasn't equipped or staffed to carry out that treatment. More troubling, the extracorporeal membrane oxygenation (ECMO) treatment—as its name implies, blood is taken out of the body, loaded with oxygen in a machine, and then immediately pumped back into the body—is most successful within eight days of a patient's being placed on a ventilator. Jeff learned of that from Lisa's intensivist, the doctor overseeing her care in the ICU. Previously, other doctors had suggested that they transfer Lisa to a hospital better equipped to serve the needs of a patient as crucially ill as she was. Jeff had tried to have Lisa transferred, but there were no beds available elsewhere.

With the news about ECMO and the window on it rapidly closing, now was the time to act. Jeff took advantage of all the resources at his disposal. Administrative delays at the hospital resulted in a request that she be taken to Emory University Hospital in Atlanta being denied. Angry but undaunted, Jeff reached out again for help, using Facebook. Remarkably, a family friend contacted Jeff, letting him know that he had a connection in Gainesville, Florida, where a bed was available. Unfortunately, Jeff was working to make it happen on a Saturday. Unable to get the needed cooperation from his health insurance provider, another opportunity was lost. Alternately praising God for presenting him with opportunities and dismayed by procedural and systemic hiccups, Jeff pressed on. He was amazed by the number of people who reached out to him to offer more possibilities. For a variety of reasons, none bore any fruit until one lead at a hospital in Macon, Georgia, did—temporarily. All the paperwork went through, but as the ambulatory team prepared to transfer her by helicopter, Lisa's blood oxygen level dropped dangerously. She never made it out of the room in the ICU at Waycross. Jeff felt that "God was at work and [I] had to trust His timing."

Jeff and Lisa had received enormous support throughout their ordeal. He credited the prayer warriors among the medical professionals and others who had seen them through to this point. A former childhood classmate had become a respected specialist at that hospital in Macon. She spoke with Jeff and delivered a sobering and necessary message: Lisa's condition was so serious that he needed to start preparing himself for the worst possible outcome. Not for the first time, he fervently prayed for God's intervention.

Lisa's condition worsened. Fluid began to build up in her body. A drug had to be administered to deal with that. Any complications, any additional drugs she had to take could weaken her to the point that she could die. Her body was performing a delicate balancing act. She had limited energy reserves to heal. Then she started to improve. A doctor expressed some hope that she might be able to survive a procedure that would enable her to be taken off the ventilator. That would alleviate one of the problems that ventilators cause: the buildup of carbon dioxide in the body, which could possibly lead to kidney failure and death. Lisa's condition improved to the point that the procedure was scheduled. However, once again her oxygen level plummeted. The doctors couldn't do the procedure with her in that condition. The ups and downs had been continuous, and in the middle of that latest descent, Jeff was reminded of just how precarious the ride was and how remarkable it was that Lisa was still alive. He spoke with one of the surgeons who was hoping to perform the procedure on Lisa. He told Jeff that he had never seen a patient come back from a drop in oxygen level to the point that Lisa had. During the follow-up meeting with Jeff, the doctors laid it on the line: Lisa's chances of surviving were very, very low. Jeff chose not to share that information with the family. He needed them to remain optimistic, to help buoy his spirits. At any time during this ordeal, that was critically important. It was especially important when the potentially lifesaving procedure had to be canceled. Still, Jeff was reminded that at least Lisa was still in the game. Four more COVID-19 patients were admitted to the small hospital. Twice during the weekend after Lisa's numbers dropped so badly, Jeff witnessed two different families clustered in the hallway, mourning the loss of a loved one.

He felt enormously sorry for them but grateful that because of God's abundant provisions, Lisa had stabilized and was now improving. Having regained some strength, she was able to provide her family with a much-needed boost. Doctors could back off on the dosage of sedatives they were giving her. She was able to interact with the family by moving her eyes. She could respond by nodding or shaking her head. When asked if she was comfortable, she shook her head forcefully. That was another bittersweet moment. Jeff was glad that she could communicate but hated to know that she was in such great pain. With alertness came greater expression of her discomfort.

Jeff had been constantly saying "Thy will be done" as part of his continual prayers. An essential part of surrendering our will to God's will is the reality that we might suffer pain as a result of accepting what God has in store for us.

On October 20, Jeff bore the brunt of that reality. Lisa was suffering from acute respiratory distress syndrome (ARDS). The tissues in her lungs had stiffened and swollen. That made it difficult for them to inflate and deflate properly. Her brain was begging for more oxygen, but even with the ventilator pumping 100 percent oxygen into her damaged lungs, her solid flesh wasn't responding properly. She faced the real possibility that her heart rate would rise to the point that she might suffer a heart attack. The doctors could only force air into her lungs at a pressure that wouldn't cause them to burst. If her blood oxygen level stayed too low, she could suffer permanent brain damage. That day, it seemed as if everything the doctors tried wasn't working.

Jeff was rushed into the room while the team worked feverishly on his wife. He was shocked to see the fixed expression on his wife's face. She had the death stare. Jeff fell to his knees alongside her bed. He asked God to spare his wife. He held her foot and said, "Please, honey, don't go! Please stay with me."

He was crying, and as he looked at the others in the room working to save his wife's life, he saw tears leaking from their eyes, too. Jeff was torn. As much as he wanted his wife to go on living, he recalled words she'd said in the past: "Just let me go. I know where I'm going and to Whom I belong." Still, he couldn't bear the thought of losing his wife. He asked the doctor if it was time for him to get family members to join him for what he expected would be her last moments on Earth.

The doctor's nod was like a punch to the solar plexus, taking away every bit of oxygen in Jeff's lungs. He called Lisa's parents, delivering the news that every parent dreads: a child isn't going to make it. He texted each of their children, letting them know the same thing. Lisa could be stabilized to the point that she could be reconnected to the ventilator. The family gathered. Individually, they went into the room to offer her comfort and say goodbye. Questions, regrets—Mama might not be there for Harper Lee's wedding—disbelief swirled in the waiting room. What was it they were waiting for? Lisa's death or her recovery?

To their great relief, it was her recovery. They had no idea how long it would last, but she somehow pulled through that latest crisis. Lisa's father, Howard, assumed the lead in encouraging his daughter to keep breathing. He'd asked Jeff what a good number was to appear on the oxygen level display. At first Jeff said seventy-five. Howard nodded. He knew his little girl, and he had always had a special relationship with her. He'd get her there. Minutes later he came out to report that Lisa was at seventy-five. What next? Eighty-five. Done.

Not done.

The episode had so weakened Lisa that her grip on life was tenuous at best. It was time for everyone to have a frank discussion about the next steps to take. Jeff could no longer protect everyone else from the truth. Lisa was in serious jeopardy, he told them. She'd been there frequently in the past. Each time she had been and had recovered, the process had taken longer and left her fewer reserves to take on the next crisis. He added that the doctors had reached the limits of the treatment options available in Waycross. They could transfer her and hope she survived the journey. They could honor the wishes that she had spelled out and let her go.

With everyone up to speed, they spoke openly, weighing the options. Jeff suggested that they reconvene in six hours. They had a heavy weight on their shoulders, and it was best to set it down for a bit and recover. While they did, Jeff once again received comfort from the presence of more friends showing up in support. At the appointed hour, everyone got a chance to speak. They took head-on what Lisa had clearly expressed in her living will: she had asked to be placed on a ventilator.

It was at that point that Jeff came up with the three-day solution. At the end of that time, it would be one full calendar month since Lisa had gone on the ventilator. Jeff believed that if in those days she built up enough strength for her to be transferred to another hospital, that was the sign that they should continue to pursue treatment options. It wasn't like asking God for a job offer, a 1972 quarter to appear, or any of the other signs and whisperings the couple had asked for or experienced over the years. The consequences were far greater than anything they'd faced before. But as they had many times in the past, Jeff believed that God had put the three-day option into his heart, and he was committed to honoring it.

It seemed as if God had recognized what they, and so many others, had hoped and prayed for. Lisa continued to improve. A bed opened up at a hospital in Savannah. Lisa appeared to be strong enough to be temporarily disconnected from the ventilator. A nurse would fly with her in the helicopter, using a manual pump to keep oxygen flowing into Lisa's lungs. Jeff gave his consent to the move. As he exited the hospital, he saw the Life Flight helicopter sitting on the ground. He shouted to the people who would be transporting his wife, letting them know he was praying for them as much as he was praying for her. He sped off in Lisa's car, wanting to be there in time to greet her in Savannah.

An understanding state trooper, having pulled Jeff over for speeding, agreed to escort the grateful husband and father to the destination. Lisa had been in great, deeply caring, and compassionate hands in Waycross. She was now being treated at a teaching hospital, one with a level-one trauma center. The doctors there told him that his wife had survived the flight without incident. The bad news was that her lungs were so bad that she would need a double lung transplant. Jeff wondered if any donor lungs would even be available during a pandemic. He also knew that double lung transplant recipients survived for only two to three years. Lastly, Lisa's living will vetoed taking extraordinary measures to save her life. The transplant option was off the table.

As Jeff later wrote, "God had answered my heart's cry by getting her here, and now I could see how very deep her need was. I began praying through my tears. 'Lord, You've been so good, now please protect her, restore her, let her live a life of strength and a testimony of Your faithfulness!'"

Doctors were trying to predict what was next. But her lungs were "baked," as they put it. And, she had suffered a stroke along the way. They had to ease her into a medically induced coma and no one could tell what level of impairment she would have when she awakened. Jeff believed that she was clearly suffering. She'd expressed her end-of-life wishes. Would she resent him if she recovered only to live out her remaining days severely debilitated and facing one medical challenge after another? What would her quality of life be like?

He engaged in ceaseless prayer. He spoke with Lisa's brother, Parker, letting him know what few options remained. The wait went on. Lisa showed no signs of responsiveness during a neurological exam. She was being examined by a variety of specialists. One of them broached the question that had been asked multiple times before: Was it time to let her go? It wasn't, Jeff decided.

Jeff later wrote, "One night, a friend sent me a recording of a sermon. I listened to the preacher say, 'Stop saying "If it's the Lord's will," when you have a burden on your heart! Be honest enough with Him and start asking for what's on your heart . . . with boldness! Speak up and say it with faith!'" I normally disavowed that type of doctrine, but in my hour of need I took courage from it and began changing my prayers with specificity that shifted my appeal to God in very particular terms. I spoke to Him as a child speaks to a parent. I wasn't bargaining with Him. I made no conditional promises. I simply began praying for Lisa in a way that I had previously been very hesitant to ask for out of a fear of disappointment. I have always known God has the ultimate say in Lisa's life, but I began telling God that I believed He would heal her in spite of what doctors had said previously. I began praying with vision and unction that was beyond words. I could see in my mind Lisa being awake and prospering. I cried with joy."

The next morning, Jeff drove back to the hospital. He sang a song from Lisa's healing playlist, "Great Are You Lord" performed by All Sons & Daughters. By the time he got to the parking lot, he was a mess, a mash-up of joy and sorrow. He made his way up to Lisa's room. A nurse was in the room when Jeff laid his jacket down. She was shocked to see Lisa's eyes tracking Jeff's movements. She let Jeff know what she'd just witnessed. Jeff was equally shocked. He moved to the other side of the bed. Lisa followed him with her eyes!

He asked if Lisa could hear him.

She nodded.

He asked if Lisa was in pain.

She shook her head.

He asked if she understood him.

A bit of irritation registered on her face; then she nodded.

That was what Jeff needed to see. That bit of sass let him know that it was the breakthrough moment. The nurse stepped out to let the doctor know about Lisa's status. Jeff remained with Lisa, telling her over and over again that he loved her. Lisa's breakthrough had come just in time. There were only twenty-four hours left of the eleven days the family had agreed to before they would take her off life support.

A disturbing bit of reality intruded at that point. Jeff asked, "Are you glad to be alive?"

Lisa shook her head. No.

As Lisa later explained, "When I was in my coma, I was being given a lot of different drugs, including fentanyl. I was in some sort of state where I was aware of my surroundings. I felt trapped. I thought I was in Hell. I was having a lot of nightmares that I could not wake up from. I couldn't separate reality from that altered state. I was in a terrible place. I dreamed twice that my son had died. Other horrible things happened. And when I woke up, I thought that those terrible things were real. I woke up into a world without my son. I woke up to a very painful reality that wasn't. But I didn't know that then."

Months later, Lisa is grateful that doctors were able to treat both her physical and mental health. She knows that Jackson didn't die and the other horrible events that terrorized her comatose state didn't happen, either. She faced a very long road to recovery. From that point, at the end of October, she faced spending months in hospitals and rehabilitation facilities.

When asked again about whether she's glad to be alive, Lisa's answer is a resounding "Yes!"

Even during those first still very difficult weeks following her recognizing Jeff, she felt that way. "Once I realized, 'Oh, I've just had COVID-19 and I'm in the hospital and I'm not in those terrible dreams anymore,' I was so happy to be alive. I could care less that I couldn't talk; I could care less that I couldn't go to the bathroom by myself. I could care less that I couldn't walk and couldn't talk. I was free from those terrible nightmares. I was just happy to be alive. And I will say this, this is a big deal. From the moment I woke up, everybody—the nurses, the doctors, Jeff—they all knew I'm somebody you better be straight with. You better tell me what's going on. So they would tell me about my loss of abilities. But they also kept saying 'You're going to get it back. You're going to get it back. This is just temporary; you're going to get it back.' And so even though my hair is my glory, I've got thick, black, dark, beautiful hair, I'm known for my hair. If my hair looks good, I don't care about my makeup or anything. But even still, they kept saying that my hair was going to grow back."

Lisa's recovery captured hearts and imaginations. She spent

fifty-nine days on a ventilator. She endured forty days in an induced coma. She survived a frontal lobe stroke.

The important thing is that she survived. She's had more to do since then, of course, but with God's help, with the help of the thousands of people who showed their support by sending cards, flowers, messages, and, most important of all, prayers, she is moving from surviving to thriving.

Another miracle she's grateful for is the healing of her relationship with her husband. "One of the best things that has happened is that my husband and I are closer than ever. We truly have a love story that has spanned time." Jeff's work-life balance has greatly improved, and their love has only grown stronger through the testing of COVID-19.

God intervened at so many points along the way to keep alive Lisa Martin, the woman who thought she didn't want to live. Though Lisa had asked God to take her, He didn't. The all-powerful, all-knowing, all-merciful God responded to the prayers of the many and not those of the wife and mother who struggled with depressive episodes at various parts of her life. He heard Lisa's words, but He understood the true meaning of her pleas to Him.

Lisa wanted what we all want. She wanted to know that she was loved. The questions that she was asking weren't so much about what she would do next with her life. They were more about whether or not she was loved. Along with that, she must have been wondering what she could do with the abundance of love that was in her heart. She was so accustomed to "close in" love that love at a distance felt strange to her. But as COVID-19 showed us all, love at a distance is not what we want: Sometimes it is all we can offer. At least, love at a remove is not the same thing as love removed.

The outpouring of affection and concern Lisa received is abundant evidence of that. The compassion and dedication of health care providers, her husband and children, friends, and strangers all reaching out in support showed her that sometimes God whispers privately to us. And other times, He shouts loud enough to penetrate illness, depression, a coma, or whatever difficulties we all face in life. No matter how bad things might get, we cannot deny that God loves us all. We can see signs of His abundant love every day.

MY NORTH STAR

Always looking to the heavens to catch a sparkle of wisdom
and love from my warrior dad.

> Even if you had ten thousand guardians in Christ,
> you do not have many fathers, for in Christ Jesus I
> became your father through the gospel. Therefore
> I urge you to imitate me.
>
> — I CORINTHIANS 4:15–16

When my father passed away on Christmas Day 2020, we lost our family's Christmas North Star. Retired Lieutenant Colonel Bobby R. Harris, the man whose grace and strength guided me and so many others, was following God's orders and dutifully transferred to Heaven. There he took his place alongside my beloved mother, Shirley. From their new command post, the two of them have continued their mission to aid God in watching over me. My father served two tours as a pilot flying combat missions over Vietnam. He went on to serve with distinction afterward, rising to the rank of lieutenant colonel. He worked under General Colin Powell in the Pentagon. To say that I loved my father and wanted to be like him doesn't quite capture our relationship. When I was a young girl, I convinced my parents to let me carry his surname as my given name. My father gave me so much more than that.

For one thing, he taught me the value of prayer. I remember him saying "People say they'll do lots of things for you. There's always one thing they say they'll do: pray. But they don't. They don't pray effectively for you. They don't even pray effectively for themselves. But you know that I will always pray without ceasing for you."

His faith was deeply tied, as everything else was, to his military service. My mother also served, unofficially, in the military. That's how it is with military families. My mom was like most spouses of our servicemen and women; when you're in the military, it's a family commitment and dedication.

My father knew and appreciated what she had contributed over the years. Without her love and support, there would have been no dad on base at Fort Monmouth in New Jersey leading a battalion. There would have been no dad on base in the Command and General Staff College at Fort Leavenworth without my mom. She was, as he called her, the greatest civilian warrior he's ever known.

As a pilot my father had to learn a lot about navigation. He flew in the days before sophisticated Global Positioning System (GPS) technology guided pilots to their targets. Equally important as reaching those targets was getting back home to the airfield. If the simple instruments in the plane failed, my father relied on a backup plan: his own senses and getting there by dead reckoning. That meant that he had to be observant of his surroundings, especially the terrain below him, and the effects the wind and other elements had on his flight path. My dad wasn't only courageous, he was smart.

Bigger picture: it was important to my father that he get back home stateside to us. But he understood that that wasn't a given, it was a gift. For any soldier, sailor, pilot, marine, or any other service member serving in combat, returning alive was a miraculous gift.

Rescue

My father was a warrior, and for any warrior on the front lines or in the skies above, waking up each day is a miracle. Warriors exist in a unique environment in which constantly someone is trying to kill them. To survive that, they need faith. In the same way that Earnestine Reese praised the Lord in the aftermath of the storm and Heather Brown, pulled from the ocean, proclaimed "God is real," my dad saw God as his protector and rescuer.

Faith was foundational to my father. He felt it was important that he recognize that and be transparent about what made him successful. He thought that every experience in life was not to be taken for granted or wasted. And so it was ingrained into me at a very early age that the deeper the struggle, the greater the revelation of just how solid faith is. My father never feared being challenged or tested. But he also knew that he was incredibly blessed and that tests were going to come. Some were by choice; others were just the products of being at war.

I don't know if it was a particular battle he fought in that developed that mindset, but he went into every engagement with the enemy with the ultimate warrior not just by his side but guiding him. War was difficult for him. He would say that the Lord doesn't want us to kill. But he understood that it was necessary sometimes. So it was very important that he truly and deeply believed in what it was he was fighting for. He loved this country. And in going to war, he felt as though he was playing an important role in this country's future. He fell in love with America's potential. He would say constantly how this nation is the greatest because of the potential it holds based on freedom and innovation. He used to say that we clothe, we love, we help more people, fight for more people than any other country on the planet. And that's still true today.

Purpose

In recent years I've heard Black men and women say, "I love my country, but my country hasn't always loved me back." My father never expressed it that way. In the 1960s, he was serving at a time when he did not have all the freedoms that we have now as people of color. But still he decided to join the battle. And he went into it confident in the rightness of the cause. Isaiah 54:17 tells us, "'No weapon forged against you shall prevail, and you will refute every tongue that accuses you. This is the heritage of the servants of the LORD, and this is their vindication from me,' declares the LORD." This tells us that God will protect the church. He will protect believers from adversaries on the battlefield where violence and force are at work.

My dad told me either you have faith that that protection is true or you don't. There's no gray area. He fought a war, and he had faith, and he did come home. And God seemed to protect him from accusing tongues as well. In the 1970s, a lot of protestors against the Vietnam War exercised their right to free speech and hurled insults at returning veterans. My father heard all kinds of accusations but was able to stay strong, focused and safe.

Throughout this book, I've covered stories of people finding their God-given purpose or what I've coined, their Divine Assignment. That enables them to see beyond the challenges of the moment to what could be. Sarah Olson wouldn't let the medical establishment define for her what a CEO should look like. She didn't let the world limit the good she could do. Len and Cherylann Gengel were not daunted by how difficult it is to make change happen in Haiti. My dad was that sort of person. He looked at a challenging world, and God gave him the vision and the courage to see beyond it.

Perseverance

This notion of belief reminds me of one of my favorite memories of my dad. We both loved the *Star Wars* movies. He was a pilot, so I suppose it was only natural. When the first movie came out in 1977, we couldn't wait to go see it. My mother declined. Storm trooper? Like, you've got to be kidding me. She joked that that particular movie was one where she wasn't willing to cross a personal line.

In any case, my father and I went, and I loved all those characters. Master Yoda has been known to say some now famous quotes throughout the *Star Wars* series. One of my favorites Yoda lines is "No! Try not. Do or do not. There is no try."

That was my father in a nutshell. He had the faith of knowing that God had given him an assignment. He was doing what he was doing for the right reasons. And later, as a lieutenant colonel, he had success. To lead people, he needed to know that there was an Ultimate Leader guiding him in his life. He led by example.

In life, you're not going to win every battle. Every mission won't be a complete success. But you keep getting up as many times as you have breath to do so. My father never said, "I'm going to try to do this." He always said, "I'm going to go do this." Sometimes he came back, and he hadn't succeeded. But he always went into things saying, "I'm doing it."

It's the same way with faith: You have to commit. You have to take the actions that your faith compels you to. You don't try to believe; YOU BELIEVE.

Like Rees Howells and his prayer warriors, my dad believed that prayer requires discipline. It is something we owe to other people. It's our weapon to fight back against the darkness. That's the same faith that motivated Gary Miracle, Ann Van Hine, and Austin Canon to keep going.

Restoration

It greatly helps to have someone who sees unending potential in you. My dad had a fierce, loving woman in his corner, championing his cause and large causes. My mom was so strong in her faith, unshakable. She had to fully commit to a spiritual knowing that a Black man going to fight was going to come back home and actually be free enough to get a job in this country. That's where America was back then, when the color of a man's skin could determine what opportunities he was offered. My mother never doubted that my dad could make the most of the opportunities available and those he envisioned for himself. Like Nancy Owen, who lived to see her mother turn to God, or Pastor Andrew Brunson, whose faith was restored in that Turkish prison, my mom prayed and believed that restoration was possible.

She always made sure that she invited civilians onto the bases where we lived in the United States and Germany. She wanted them to see what military life was like, but she also wanted them to see a common denominator between the races that were so at odds in the 1960s, when I was born. She used to pray, "Let me be a light." At her funeral in 2016, two days before Thanksgiving, as part of my eulogy to her, I sang "This Little Light of Mine" as a tribute to her. That's not me. I don't normally do that kind of thing. I don't put myself front and center at a church pulpit and sing a hymn. But it was a song for my mom to show her that her lesson to me and my sister, Annissa, was well understood. "Let your light shine before others, that they may see your good deeds and glorify your Father in heaven." (Matthew 5:16) That's what both my parents did for me, for the world, and for our Father.

Mark 10:45 tells us, "For even the Son of Man did not come not to be served, but to serve, and to give his life as a ransom for many." Not that anyone who serves in the military can be fully comparable to Jesus Christ, but that instruction is much in keeping with the desire to be of service and to know one's place in the order of things. We can all be a light. It's an incredible light inside us that connects us with the Lord. It helps us do important things together. The light of faith can move mountains.

My father's journey into the upper echelons of the Defense Department required a lot of intelligence, a lot of courage, and a lot of faith—in himself, in my mother, and in God. Put that all together, and you've got a potent combination of forces that can, and did, move mountains. Yet if I hadn't been paying attention and sometimes prodding him to talk with me about his experiences, I might not have known about his mountain moving. Like a lot of men and women who served in our nation's armed forces, my father did so quietly. In his case, it wasn't because he felt guilt or shame for what he'd done. He was just humble. He saw boasting as a sign of weakness and insecurity. That didn't mean that he rejected accolades. It was enough to get more metal on your chest, he used to say, that signified that you were moving up the ranks. Let the medals and service ribbons do the talking. I can't ever imagine my father bellying up to a bar to drink a beer and share a boast. That was never my dad. I wasn't raised to do that, either.

Healing

Humility is such a basic faith concept. After my father's passing, my sister and I collected his personal favorites and keepsakes. Among the items which I kept was his Bible. Upon opening it, little folded pieces of paper began falling out. My father had marked up certain passages and had inserted handwritten notes in between some of the pages. At the time, I couldn't look through it carefully. It was too painful a reminder of loss. But time passes, and needs arise. And I came across this passage from the book of Jeremiah that my father noted:

> This is what the LORD says: "Let not the wise
> boast of their wisdom or the strong boast of their
> strength or the rich boast of their riches, but let the
> one who boasts boast about this: that they have the
> understanding to know me, that I am the LORD,
> who exercises kindness, justice and righteousness
> on earth, for in these I delight," declares the LORD.
>
> (JEREMIAH 9:23–24)

The Bible is filled with verses about humility. Proverbs 22:4 tells us, "Humility is the fear of the LORD; its wages are riches and honor and life." My father was never in it for the riches. He was there to be of service. The honors came, and it's important to note how often the Bible places humility before honor. "Humble yourselves before the LORD, and he will lift you up." (James 4:10) And in Proverbs again, this time 18:12: "Before a downfall the heart is haughty, but humility comes before honor." Psalm 149:4 reads, "For the LORD takes delight in his people; he crowns the humble with victory."

I also remember, at one point in my life, my father talking about how to handle successes. When you win, he said, when you have victories, it is sometimes hard to remind yourself that it's not you doing it. As humans our success is always built upon the backs of others. Our victories are only accomplished through God. That's why you have to be humble.

It may be too easy to see in my father's earliest days a simple rationale for why he believed it was important to be quiet and respectful. He came from modest means, growing up poor in east Texas. He was poor in resources but rich in intellectual gifts and will. Dad taught himself to read before he entered grade school. He was an exceptional student throughout his educational life; not that as a young man he would have ever wanted to brag about himself and his accomplishments—he wouldn't have been able to even if he'd felt compelled to do so. My father's vocal cords were underdeveloped. As a result, he couldn't speak words until he was thirteen years old. He made nearly no sound. Can you imagine what it must have been like not to be able to fully express himself until that age? That he succeeded in school despite not being able to speak is remarkable, and I believe that it helped shape his views about the importance of listening. I mentioned that in the introduction, but it's important to remind ourselves of the necessity of this skill and the role it plays in our faith and in our prayers: "Your word is a lamp for my feet, a light on my path." (Psalm 119:105)

Dad told me this about his approach to prayer: "I really try not to talk too much. I just listen. Stop telling God what to do, and just listen. I remember a time when I really couldn't talk and it worked well for me, so try it."

And I did it. And I continue to listen for what the Lord wants me to hear . . . and do next.

True Warriors

I also saw an incredible dichotomy in my father that he somehow reconciled. He was one of the kindest people I've ever known—but he also had a killer instinct that you'd have been well advised not to set in motion. How he managed to be both of those things was incredible to observe. I've heard special forces members talk about this. They are true warriors, and in one moment they could be taking out a bad guy and the next assisting someone to cross the street. That's the type of mentality and personal conduct they have to develop in themselves. And it's that ability to be in control and to understand what needs to be done to be of service in all ways that sets true warriors apart from the rest of us.

My mother and father were both warriors in defense of this country and in defense of their faith. Biblical stories of war and warriors abound. The most recognized warrior in the Bible is King David. He rose from a simple shepherd boy to the man who would triumph over the Philistine giant Goliath. God chose

David, because David was a "man after His own heart." God selected him to succeed Saul, the first man selected to be the king of Israel.

Saul seemed to the people of Israel to be the perfect man to become the warrior-king they needed. But he was a perfect king only on the surface. Though he was described as tall and handsome (1 Samuel 9:2), when he was called to be king, he hid away among the supplies (1 Samuel 10:22). People had to go looking for him. He was paranoid and proud, reluctant to listen to God, which made him ineffective. Saul had greater faith in himself than he did in the Lord. His arrogance, his refusal to trust God, and his disobedience led to his downfall.

David was different. He wasn't what anyone would have expected a king to look like—a young, ruddy-faced shepherd. But God knew David's heart. Very often we use the word "heart" in place of the word "courage." People we say have great "heart" are resilient. They are tough. They don't give up. But we also use that same expression "has a great heart," to describe someone who is compassionate, kind, and generous. That one expression bridges the gap between the two sides of the warrior nature. It took great courage for David to take on Goliath. Not only was he outsized by the giant, he was underarmored. How many of us would be willing to take on a weapon-wielding foe with a sling and some rocks? How many of us would credit God for a success like the one that David experienced? He carried his courage, his faith, and his humility forward from that first great accomplishment to establish himself as a warrior-ruler.

David also remained compassionate and discerning. Saul constantly threatened David's life. David had the chance to kill Saul, but he elected to spare him. David understood and accepted his place in the order of things. He remained respectful of Saul and his role as the man that God had chosen as king. He also deeply respected God's words and actions. It wasn't up to him to take Saul's life. It wasn't up to him to usurp the king. David knew that God had chosen him to be the next king, but he trusted God and remained obedient to Him. He would wait. He would be patient. He would wait for God to settle the matter.

David was constantly writing poems and prayers to God. In fighting Goliath he exemplified courage and perseverance, but his humility is striking. He compares himself to a vulnerable child. Imagine the arrogant Saul writing these words—it's impossible!

> My heart is not proud, LORD, my eyes are not haughty; I do not concern myself with great matters or things too wonderful for me.
>
> But I have calmed and quieted myself, I am like a weaned child with its mother; like a weaned child I am content.
>
> —PSALM 131:1–2

David truly exemplifies what it means to be a person of faith. His profound love of God, humility, trust, ability to forgive and ask for forgiveness are all attributes that make David a model for how we should conduct our lives. I see in him many of the characteristics that my father and mother had and demonstrated for me throughout their lives.

Through writing this book, it's opened my eyes further about how much prayer reminds us of our weakness and fallibility. Every time I pray, it's an admission to God that I need Him.

Jesus is the ultimate prayer warrior. From the outset, He knew what His assigned mission would be. He knew that He would have to pay the ultimate sacrifice. As part of His dual nature as human being and divine being, He would feel the pain of persecution and crucifixion. But He still cried out to God in prayer, at His weakest moment. Matthew captures one of the most moving stories in the New Testament when Jesus goes to the Garden of Gethsemane to pray:

> Then Jesus went with his disciples to a place called Gethsemane, and He said to them, "Sit here while I go over there and pray." He took Peter and the two sons of Zebedee along with him, and he began to be sorrowful and troubled. Then he said to them, "My soul is overwhelmed with sorrow to the point of death. Stay here and keep watch with me."
>
> Going a little farther, he fell with his face to the ground and prayed, "My Father, if it is possible, may this cup be taken from me. Yet not as I will, but as you will."
>
> —MATTHEW 26:36–39

Jesus prayed, and God heard his son's prayers:

> An angel from heaven appeared to him and strengthened him. And being in anguish, he prayed more earnestly, and his sweat was like drops of blood falling to the ground.
>
> —LUKE 22:43–44

After a time, Jesus gathered himself. His strength, His courage, and His faith carried Him forward:

> Then he returned to his disciples and found them
> sleeping. "Couldn't you men keep watch with me
> for one hour?" he asked Peter. "Watch and pray so
> that you will not fall into temptation. The spirit is
> willing, but the flesh is weak."
>
> —MATTHEW 26:40–41

His disciples' humanity was fully on display. Could we have done any better in those circumstances? They'd endured a long and tiring day. They did not know what was at stake. They didn't fully comprehend every aspect of the mission that Jesus had in mind for them. They didn't know the temptation they would have to endure. They weren't fully aware of the battle they would have to wage against Satan.

Twice more Jesus went back to pray alone, asking that this cup be taken from him. He said his final prayer: "May your will be done."

Moments later he was arrested. Hours later he was tried, crucified, and buried.

"May your will be done."

Even Jesus needed to pray. It was part of the example He was setting for us. In our weakest moments, we must turn to the Father.

I believe that my dad had that concept in his mind many times over the course of his life. In many senses, it fits the bill for the type of prayer he encouraged me to make: don't talk too much; listen. The Bible doesn't tell us what God said in response to Jesus's request. He remained silent. And sometimes in our lives, God will also be silent. He won't talk too much, but in his silence we have our answer. He has told us many times what our mission is. He's provided commandments to guide our actions. If we listen, if we remain open, if we remain vigilant, we will accomplish the mission He has tasked us all with. On a more personal level, God has assigned us each a role to play in this life. I love my Divine Assignment, which is to assist other people tell their stories and to disseminate those lived experiences to teach others how best to survive, thrive, and reap fulfilled lives.

That was the mission I planned and undertook in writing this book. It is the mission that I hope to accomplish every day in my role in television news. I have faith, and I pray that it is pleasing to God.

My hope is that for all of you, the same is real and active in your life, that you find joy and satisfaction in your life and your work, that you are able to glorify God in all things, that the miracle of our creation continues to please the Lord. May God's will be done through you—and may your prayers bring you closer to Him. Amen.

ACKNOWLEDGMENTS

I believe that the best books have the power to transform lives. So, I consider myself nineteen-times blessed that the individuals whose stories I was privileged to share had that effect on me. I have prayed throughout my life. But as a result of what I learned in writing this book, I now believe more firmly than ever in the power of prayer, especially when praying for others. It's a true sign that my own faith walk is growing.

I'm indebted to all of those who contributed their experiences, their joys, their sorrows, their moments of doubt, their moments of unshakable faith, and their testimony. God is indeed great. I've seen Him move through the lived experience of these individuals. And I'm eternally grateful to Him and to them for the exposure to the miraculous powers of their individual and collective grace, prayer, and faith.

Humbly, I say thank you to each of them and you, the reader, for sharing this experience with me. I also want to thank the many people who I know have prayed for me over the course of my life.

Never before have I felt the active presence of those words and thoughts to so great a degree, and I vow to be even more active in sharing the power of prayer as an intercessor to those around me and afar.

From those I may never see again or meet to the people closest to me, please know that this path along my faith walk has been amazing!

My fiercest and most loving support team are always my family. They allow me to immerse myself in my divine assignments and career dreams. At Fox News, along with our CEO Suzanne Scott, whose encouragement was key, Jason Klarman, the president of Fox Nation and executive vice president of marketing at Fox News, were instrumental in forming the successful partnership with HarperCollins Publishers. Also at Fox, Michael Tammero, the senior vice president of marketing and brand strategy, contributed in so many ways to the handling of various day-to-day aspects of seeing a book through from conception to publication. Similarly, at HarperCollins, my editor, Hannah Long, was invaluable. The only qualities that eclipse Hannah's keen editorial vision are her grace and generosity. I also want to thank James Neidhardt, who stepped in at the last minute to assist in the final push across the finish line. And my special appreciation to HarperCollins publicist Theresa Dooley and designer Joanne O'Neill who designed just the right cover for my book about moving mountains through prayer.

The written word is only a gift if it can be read. Thank you to all of you for making that possible.

NOTES

1. Christopher Brito, "Teens Stranded at Sea Cried Out to God for Help. Then a Boat Named 'Amen' Rescued Them," CBS News, May 3, 2019, https://www.cbsnews.com/news/boat-named-amen-florida-swimming tyler-smith-heather-brown/.
2. Ibid.
3. "Teens Stranded in Ocean Cry Out to God for Help, Get Rescued by Boat Named 'Amen,'" FaithPot, March 3, 2022, https://www.faithpot .com/amen-boat-rescues-teens-stranded-in-ocean/.
4. "Frequently Asked Questions About ECT," Johns Hopkins Medicine, https://www.hopkinsmedicine.org/psychiatry/specialty_areas/brain _stimulation/ect/faq_ect.html.
5. Greg Garrison, "The Secret of Earnestine's Prayer Closet," AL.com, February 28, 2020, https://www.al.com/life/2019/03/the-secret-of -earnestines-prayer-closet-prayer-works-in-other-rooms-too.html.
6. Katie Kamin, "'Tell God Thank You': Lee Co. Tornado Survivor Still Praising God a Year Later," WTVM, March 8, 2020, https://www .wtvm.com/2020/03/09/tell-god-thank-you-lee-co-tornado-survivor-still -praising-god-year-later/.
7. Garrison, "The Secret of Earnestine's Prayer Closet."
8. Ibid.

9. "Religious Landscape Study: State," Pew Research Center, https://www
.pewresearch.org/religion/religious-landscape-study/state/.

10. Garrison, "The Secret of Earnestine's Prayer Closet."

11. Kamin, "'Tell God Thank You.'"

12. 11Alive, "She Lost Her Home in the Alabama Tornadoes. Her Photos
Showed Up All over Georgia," YouTube, March 21, 2019, https://www
.youtube.com/watch?v=6Bvws5w2uh4&list=PLxSDPGC2EVp
-Yi8yZPj9keae59HqJ551E&index=54.

13. Elizabeth White, "Earnestine Reese, Who Became Famous for her Prayer
Closet Is Welcomed Home," Facebook, https://www.facebook.com/
watch/live/?ref=watch_permalink&v=505410050092052.

14. Garrison, "The Secret of Earnestine's Prayer Closet."

15. Elizabeth White, "Earnestine Reese, Who Became Famous for her Prayer
Closet Is Welcomed Home," Facebook, https://www.facebook.com
/watch/live/?ref=watch_permalink&v=505410050092052.

16. Ibid.

17. Much of this story is based on the account of Msgr. James H. O'Neill,
"The True Story of the Patton Prayer," *Review of the News*, October 6,
1971, 35–39, http://pattonhq.com/prayer.html, which first appeared as a
government document in 1950.

18. Associated Press, "AP Was There: Battle of the Bulge," Associated
Press, December 22, 2020, https://apnews.com/article/entertainment
-europe-world-war-ii-b7a34f2ee194e179bd0203ef8bcafa9f.

19. Stephanie Hertzenberg, "3 Times Prayer Changed History," Beliefnet,
https://www.beliefnet.com/inspiration/3-times-prayer-changed-history
.aspx.

20. "Battle of the Bulge," History.com.

21. John S. D. Eisenhower, *The Bitter Woods: The Battle of the Bulge* (New York:
Putnam, 1969), 457.

22. Author's interview with Benjamin Patton, June 13, 2022.

23. O'Neill, "The True Story of the Patton Prayer."

24. Caitlin Hu, "Ten years after a devastating earthquake, some Haitians
say they're losing hope," CNN, January 13, 2020, https://www.cnn

.com/2020/01/12/world/haiti-earthquake-ten-years-anniversary-intl/index.html.

25. Opening anecdote is a dramatization based on quotes from George Washington Carver's interview with "W.W. Wheeler" (Wheeler McMillen), "'Great Creator,' *I Said, '*Why Did You Make the Peanut?'" *Farm and Fireside*, Nov. 1928, 8. Sourced from the archives of the New York Public Library on July 14, 2022.

26. Christina Vella, *George Washington Carver: A Life* (Baton Rouge: Louisiana State University Press, 2015), 15–16.

27. Ibid., 90.

28. Gary R. Kremer (ed.), *George Washington Carver in His Own Words* (Columbia, MO: University of Missouri, 1987), 128.

29. W.W. Wheeler (Wheeler McMillen), "'Great Creator,' *I Said, '*Why Did You Make the Peanut?'" *Farm and Fireside*, Nov. 1928, 8.

30. Ibid.

31. Perry, *George Washington Carver*, 155.

32. Dramatization based on *Hearings on General Tariff Revision Before the Committee on Ways and Means, House of Representatives* (Washington, DC: Government Printing Office, 1921), 2070–77, https://www.google.com/books/edition/Schedule_F/ijcMAQAAMAAJ.

33. Ibid. 2077.

34. Perry, 108.

35. George Washington Carver, *George Washington Carver: In His Own Words*, edited by Gary R. Kremer (Columbia, MO: University of Missouri Press, 1987), 143.

36. "Turkey's failed coup attempt: All you need to know," Al Jazeera, July 15, 2017, https://www.aljazeera.com/news/2017/7/15/turkeys-failed-coup-attempt-all-you-need-to-know.

37. Interview with Samuel Howells, "The Intercessor: Rees Howells," JerusalemChannel, YouTube, August 24, 2018. https://youtu.be/Qv_zzh5XilU.

38. Norman Grubb, *Rees Howells, Intercessor* (Fort Washington, PA: CLC Publications, 1952), 24–27.

39. Interview with Samuel Howells, "The Intercessor: Rees Howells," JerusalemChannel, YouTube, August 24, 2018. https://youtu.be/Qv_zzh5XilU.

40. David Martyn Lloyd-Jones, Studies in the Sermon on the Mount (Grand Rapids: Wm. B. Eerdmans Publishing Company: 1984), 322.

41. Norman Grubb, *Rees Howells, Intercessor* (Fort Washington, PA: CLC Publications, 1952), Kindle edition, 150.

42. Interview with Samuel Howells, "The Intercessor: Rees Howells," JerusalemChannel, YouTube, August 24, 2018. https://youtu.be/Qv_zzh5XilU.

43. Ibid., 149.

44. Nevile Henderson, *Failure of a Mission: Berlin 1937–1939* (New York: G. P. Putnam's Sons, 1940), 225, 252.

45. Grubb, *Rees Howells*, 172.

46. Interview with Ruth Williams, "The Intercessor: Rees Howells," JerusalemChannel, YouTube, August 24, 2018. https://youtu.be/Qv_zzh5XilU.

47. Winston S. Churchill, *The Second World War* (London: Cassell, 1959), 351.

48. Viktor Andreevich Kravchenko, *I Chose Freedom: The Personal and Political Life of a Soviet Official* (New York: Scribner, 1946), 377.

49. Grubb, *Rees Howells*, 180.

50. Ibid., 165.

51. Ann Van Hine, *Pieces Falling* (United States: Illumify Media, 2021), 209.

52. Excerpted from the manuscript of "SHUG: A Story of Restoration" by Jeff Martin.

53. Ibid.

54. Ibid.

INDEX

ABOUT THE AUTHOR

Harris Faulkner is a six-time Emmy award–winning anchor and nationally bestselling author of *9 Rules of Engagement: A Military Brat's Guide to Life and Success*. Faulkner joined FOX News Channel in 2005 and currently anchors *The Faulkner Focus* and serves as the co-anchor of *Outnumbered*. Outside of her work as a journalist, Faulkner is a motivational speaker, writer, and philanthropist. She resides in New Jersey with husband Tony Berlin and their two daughters.